PARENTAL
BLOOPERS

VOL. 01

PARENTAL BLOOPERS

VOL. 01

LEARNING TO LAUGH WHILE PARENTING

Authored by

LOYSON PAES

Penman Books

Office No. 303, Kumar House Building,
D Block, Central Market, Opp PVR Cinema,
Prashant Vihar, Delhi 110085, India
Website: www.penmanbooks.com
Email: publish@penmanbooks.com

First Published by Penman Books 2019
Copyright © Loyson Paes 2019
All Rights Reserved.

Title: Parental Bloopers
Price: ₹199 | $6.6
ISBN: 978-93-89024-24-1

*To the two little pumplings, Rishaan and Anaira,
without whom the content of this book would never have
manifested; without whom this book would have been
released much earlier.*

*To my very pretty wife, Soumya who stood by me
even though I wasn't there but was in some corner
of the house ferociously writing into the laptop.*

*Darling, I don't know if it is old age already but
I still stand by the promise of growing old with you.
We will rock together.*

Preface

I still remember the day, I knelt in front of the altar with my very pretty wife by my side. She looked so beautiful and I felt my heart skipped a beat every time I brushed my gaze on her glowing face. It was the day the parish priest in the little town of Cuncolim in South Goa had just pronounced us man and wife.

For both of us, marriage was a huge task accomplished and an achievement in itself given the fact that we belonged to two very different cultures and religions. I remember a lot of naysayers telling me that life will change after marriage. That all the love will diminish when reality and finances settle in. But apart from a few arguments here and there and a few fist fights (sometimes beyond) being thrown in to dramatise the whole relationship, a lot otherwise was just the usual. And it continued to be the usual till that one day! That one day after which, life for Soumya and me was never meant to be the same.

That day when I was parading up and down against the white wall of the nursing home's corridor, my brother-in-law was busy making a video in order to record the expressions that were expected to be expressed. With all the storm of thoughts that was swirling in my mind, I was hardly cognitive of his presence; leave alone the video. I could constantly, feel a lump in my throat that I'm sure was my heart. The phrase 'having the heart in the mouth' was actually experienced by someone before me who contributed this phrase to the rest of mankind.

Each time, I noticed someone coming out of the operation theatre, the lump in my throat stopped working and moved up by an inch. An endoscopy would have proven this fact.

And then there it was - the moment that I had been waiting for the last nine months. The first time I heard the cry, it was obviously like music to the soul. I didn't know that the cry would be repeated so often that the feeling of 'music to the soul' was about to change to the 'Sunday evening Doordarshan music' pretty soon.

But for now, there he was! Wrapped in a white cloth. Looking absolutely divine. The cry was different from the usual but who cared. All that mattered at that point in time was... He had arrived. My son. Soumya's and my first offspring.

Whoever said that *'Life changes after marriage!'* Life actually changes after kids.

The next three hundred and sixty five days witnessed our life go through all kinds of ups and downs. Our love for each other and our fights with each other were like never before. The relationship had reached extreme weathers.

All because of the presence of one tiny little human being in our life. It was an obsession that we wanted everything to be perfect for him. We wanted the cleanest of the cleans and the healthiest of the healthy. And we strived and struggled our butts off to ensure that he got that. We had given up on our sleep, our relationships, our friendships, everything, just to ensure that this one little soul was happy in life!

But then, was he really happy?

Just when life had started settling down for us *or so we had badly wanted to imagine*, we had no clue of another similar day coming to revive that ruckus in our life! The day when both of us helplessly sat on the bed and held hands and cried. We didn't know if we were prepared and at the same time, we couldn't imagine taking a step that would leave us with a sense of remorse for the rest of our beautifully planned lives.

Over the next few days however, it was the pain of regret that witnessed victory as we decided that our son deserved a sibling. There was no turning back since then and today as we look back we are glad that we decided what we decided. However, from a learning from life's situation's perspective, I believe a slightly different outlook toward parenting could have worked a charm in our life.

For starters, we took parenting too seriously and in the bargain, we never really stopped to enjoy the whole process to sit back and watch the kids grow. A child is the epitome of innocence and steers the way we steer them. There were so many messages related to kids that came to us through various platforms and we felt that we need to try them all. Poor kids, I must say! They became the Guinea pigs of all the experiments that we tried and tested on them.

The very subtle message that this book delivers is that while parenting these days can really be stressful, let's also sit back and watch our little brats grow and talk and play. Kids are at their best when left to themselves.

Let's together learn to laugh while parenting!

Introduction

When I was a child, my parents had taken the pains of noting down every little milestone and achievement all the way from my birth till about 5 years or so as much as I can remember. Even as a little boy, I was so impressed with this, that I had made a vow to myself that when I have a child of my own, I would love to write down similar notes about him / her so that they would also remember me for what I had done.

Fast forward it to two decades into the future, I started writing similar notes when we first got the news of the arrival of a little baby into our lives. Throughout the remainder of the six months that we were aware of his presence in the womb, I began writing a little black diary about the several beautiful things that were going on around us. The pregnancy cravings, the doctor visits, the scans and their reports, the excitement in the family, et al was neatly recorded; with me *selfishly* practising my writing skills in the bargain.

I wrote and wrote and continued to write till the day Rishaan, my son was born!

One year later when we started settling down with little Rishaan in our life, the cleanliness obsessed Soumya decided to clear up one of the cupboards to make space for baby clothes. And there it was – staring back at us. The little black diary had gathered up dust over the last four quarters.

It suddenly dawned on me that I had not noted anything about Rishaan's baby milestones and young achievements as was decided by the little 'me' two decades back. Just when I decided that I would rectify this mistake by starting to write once again, *phew*! Anaira, my daughter happened! The book was packed and found its dwelling in one of the cupboards once again; this time for a much longer time.

As days passed into weeks and weeks turned into months, the guilt feeling about not noting any milestones slowly faded away and we were back to our normal course of life. Every evening, when I was back from a tiring day at work, Soumya would give me an update about all the events and conversations that the kids would have with her. I found the kids to be unusually hilarious and I slowly started looking forward to the updates by Soumya. The kids would also perch themselves by our side and this became a normal course of daily routine for us; our little version of family time in the ever increasing attention demands that various items in life posed.

I slowly took to writing down the situational humour on social platforms with a simple objective of having this documented so that Soumya and I would be able to recollect the events and laugh during our old age. However, as time beautifully passed by, we had a little community of *'fan following'* for the jokes and the little characters that Rishaan and Anaira stood for. I wont give out those character descriptions and paint your imagination as yet but will let you imagine for yourself. I came to call it the *'Joke Factory Series'* as some of our friends and relatives famously know of it.

But like they say, time helps you realise a lot of things in life and one day when Rishaan and Anaira were about their current ages, six and four respectively, Soumya had been to see a colleague who had delivered a baby about a couple of months ago. And when she came back, she couldn't stop talking about how lovely the baby was and all the cute things that the baby did. We continued to talk late into the night about how we missed all the tiny growth years of our own babies only because we were so focussed on what they should eat and how clean the floor should be before we could let them down or how the dishes we used for them needed to be sterilised and how they need to get the right nutrition and what not! We hadn't taken the time out to sit down and enjoy the pranks of the kids by staying present and stop worrying about the future.

We suddenly realised that the 'Joke Factory Series' was a gateway for us to relive and enjoy all those moments once again. But then things could have been different if we had chosen to worry lesser and laugh and play more with the kids.

We wish we had learnt to laugh while parenting!

Soumya and I have made a conscious effort to enjoy the present and stay focussed on this lesson that we have learnt after about close to six years of parenting. The book offers a range of innocent jokes that Rishaan and Anaira have cracked over a period of their life on earth and this is what provides Soumya and me our daily dose of laughter therapy amongst the many challenges that parenting these days has in store for the bravest of the brave.

So, sit back and relax whilst you enjoy this book filled with lots of innocence and child fuzzy logic that will make you go, 'Awwww!'

Contents

The Logical Child

"Only a child sees things with perfect clarity, because it hasn't developed all those filters that prevent us from seeing things that we don't expect to see."

—**Douglas Adams**

Pet for the home!

We all know that kids love pets and there is a very strong bond of love and loyalty that can be demonstrated by a pet rather than the theory of these subjects by parents.

However for us, thinking of getting another pet home when there were already enough pets…. errr…. sorry, chaos at home was unreasonable and hence it was clear between Soumya and I that we get one, only when the kids are able to take care of it.

So the other day, after looking at one of the apartment owner's dog, Rishaan finally spoke up.

Rishaan: Mamma, can we get a dog at our home?

Soumya: Yes we can. But you will take care of it?

Rishaan: (getting excited) Yes Mamma.

Soumya: Nice and you will take it for a walk every day?

Rishaan: (even more excited) Yes Mamma!!

Soumya: Great and you will clean the potty also?

Rishaan: Why? Dada is there no!

Grrrrrrr! Years back, a promise that *I will be the one cleaning the baby poop* had got Soumya to say a 'yes' to our relationship. But now, pet's poop as well?

Show me!

The sudden absence of certain conveniences in our life makes us realise the importance of them, especially when it is something that enables your morning routine.

So this one morning, there was no power at home. The kids had to take their bath and we were all handicapped without electricity, which is otherwise taken so much for granted. For some strange reason, Anaira had a strong feeling that we were planning to give her a head bath (Anaira hates head bath as much as 'hate' hates love)

Anaira: (on the verge of crying) Don't want head bath!

Soumya: (from inside the kitchen) We don't think you will get body bath also today!

Anaira: Huh?

At that moment, power returned!

Me: Ah, power's back!

Anaira: Where, show me?

Somewhere in the heavens, Benjamin Franklin and Michael Faraday scratched their heads on this one.

It's in my hand!

Soumya and I have come up with a classic method of rewards and recognition for the babies at home. Each achievement, small or big, is rewarded with a star on their respective Post-it stuck on the wall. This has led to a rise in achievements and something to look forward to by the kids.

So this morning Rishaan, Anaira and I were lazing on the sofa.

Anaira: Dada, I was a good girl today. You will give me a star? (Good girl smile follows)

Rishaan: No Dada. She scratched me in the morning. (Showing me a molecular something that could potentially qualify as a scratch)

Anaira: (pissed) Rishaan, don't tell all that!

Me: Don't worry Anaira! The decision is ultimately mine. Your star is in my hand.

Anaira: (surprised and opening my palm) Where? You telling lies! It's not there!

I decided immediately that I adopt the 'Maun Vrath!'

Look who's talking!

The last thing for a parent in this already chaotic world is for the child to create a ruckus by crying out loud. Whenever Rishaan or Anaira cries in the house, I immediately shout out in an attempt to create an awareness and shake them up.

Me: Who is that crying in our house? Dada does not like crying babies!

Inspite of that, Anaira continued to cry for a while before coming to a stop when she noticed that nobody seemed to bother. However, it looked like it was Rishaan's turn in a few minutes from there. By then I guess, Anaira was in a better mood and was in the other bedroom. Before I could, she shouted out!

Anaira: Aey, who is *clying* in this house? Dada does not like anyone *clying* no?

Soumya: (looking at me and speaking slowly) Look who's talking!

Anaira: (not wanting to let go of a potential compliment) Mamma, I am talking! (Smiles a good girl smile)

In the midst of the laughter that followed, Rishaan's cry for attention fell on deaf ears.

Dentist (Part 3)

Because I had not wanted the kids to create ruckus at the plush reception of the dentist, I had warned Rishaan and Anaira that if they make too much noise, then the dentist will check their teeth and if she sees their teeth, she will pull them off. So the babies were in their best behaviour for a whole of seven minutes.

After that, the decibel level gently ascended. I kept reminding them but slowly I could see a deaf ear being turned to me.

The dentist however, seemed to enjoy their company and their questions. So she got them some goodies and they were very happy. But then she said something that made Rishaan suspicious.

Dentist: You guys are so cute. Please keep coming here.

Rishaan: (tensed) Why?

A moment of staring later, the dentist saw that Rishaan indeed had a point.

God knows!

Since the time Soumya and I became parents, we keep talking about the days before the kids. Life was so peaceful and relaxed. If we decided that we want to sleep, we could just go to sleep. If we decided to go out, we could just go out. If we decided not to cook, we just wouldn't cook. Now however, ah! Lets not talk about it. The positive side of me can only come up with one conclusion: Kids discipline parents these days more than the other way around.

The other day, just as we were about to retire after a long tiring day, 'Queen' Anaira suddenly decided that her pants were not good enough to go to sleep with and that she should change them. Having no option as a father, sleepily, I led the high energy lass to her cupboard and three minutes of delayed selection later, she decided her favourite pair.

She wanted to put on the pants herself and as expected, she put the pants the other way around. So a frustrated Soumya spoke up.

Soumya: Anaira, you don't have brains or what?

Anaira: (innocently) No!

Me: (Tired, yet a Father) Anaira, say yes, I have!

Anaira: Yes mamma! I have!

Soumya: (googly) And where is your brain?

Anaira: (inverting her lips) God knows!

There are definitely certain situations in life to which only God has the answer and no one else. A lot of those situations revolve around kids.

Coins

Anaira was playing her favourite game - counting coins! Soumya had given her a piggy bank purse after a lot of puppy faces from the little Anaira. Soumya was not convinced with this. For her, the fear was that the small sized coins were not meant for human consumption!

Every time Soumya would come out of the kitchen to ensure that the five coins were visible in plain sight and would go back satisfied. But this one time, she stood transfixed. Her worst nightmare was just about to come true - Two coins were missing!

Soumya: (alarmed) Anaira where are the two coins?

Anaira: Huh? (starts counting sloooowly - 1.... 2... 3) Thlee coins are there!

Soumya: (even more panicked) Anaira, I need those two coins.

Anaira: Wait, I will get from the purse. Lotsa coins are there.

Soumya: (losing it) ANAIRA THERE WERE FIVE COINS. NOW ONLY THREE ARE THERE. WHERE ARE TWO MORE COINS?

Anaira (as calm as the sea) Wait, I will get from the purse! You be here.

Just when Soumya had the thought of getting her to puke, Anaira got up and there right under her bum, two shining coins stared back at Soumya. Phew!

No! I good GIRL!

Rishaan was creating a ruckus to go for bath and hence as a responsible father, I decided that it was my heavenly duty to suppress my anger and lighten up the situation.

I decided to take control rather than be a victim. When you have a son and a daughter, competition is key and is a solution to almost all the problems that a parent faces. I decided to involve an unknowing Anaira in my act. In order to get their attention, I suddenly jumped and stood up.

Me: Now I will show you how good boys behave. They first stand up and say, I want to take a bath.' Then they run like this (demonstrating) and get their towel and then say 'I am ready!'

I looked at them. Both seemed totally unimpressed. Now it was time for Anaira to be brought into the main act of the scene.

Me: (looking at Anaira) Anaira, wouldn't you want to be a good boy? (Oh! Oh! But the mistake was already done)

Anaira: (slapping her forehead) No, I good 'girl'.

I gave up. Through howls and screams, Rishaan was pulled across the hall to the bathroom for his cleansing.

Where is Salman Khan?

The 'Bajrangi Bhaijaan' movie witnessed a passionate four year old son and a thirty something father shed tears together. In the same house, a very practical Anaira and Soumya shared a laugh and poked jokes over the crying men.

After a while, Anaira walked into the play room to spend sometime. Meanwhile, the movie got over and the channel aired the next movie 'Ong Bak', a Chinese movie that featured mud slushed men climb a tree.

Unaware that the movie had changed, Anaira walked in coolly after putting her doll to sleep and gracefully seated herself on the sofa. She watched the movie for a minute and she suddenly sat upright wanting to ask a question.

Anaira: Aey, where is Shalman Khan?

Its so beautiful that kids see absolutely no difference between the different ethnicities around the world.

Diaper pehalwan

After you are married and have kids, going out is not as easy as going out when you are a bachelor. First you decide what the kids have to wear, then the kids throw tantrums that they don't want to wear that and want to wear something else. Then you go back, sometimes you take them to the cupboard and after a few million seconds, they decide what they want to wear, then you dress them up amidst all the running around, fun and frolic. Just when you are tired and you feel like sitting down, you realise that you also have to dress up. Phew! Lots more than just this but for setting the context, this will do for now.

We had decided to go out to the mall and we were beginning to start the whole process. Our estimated time from taking a decision to go out to actually going out is around 45 minutes. So the 45 minute process had begun.

As I opened the door to the bedroom, Soumya was getting the kids ready to go out. Anaira had just put on her diaper.

Me: (in a teasing way) What re, chaddi pehalwan? Anaira: (covering her mouth with her little palms and laughing) No, diaper pehalwan!

I was never corrected with such striking logic by a baby till that date… Or no, that one day… Oh and another….

Many

Soumya and I were trying to clear up old unnecessary files on the laptop when we stumbled upon Anaira's first birthday pictures (In Anaira's baby language, 'pichkurs')

Needless to say, we forgot all about the clearing up and we got engrossed in the memories we had created then. Loud laughter, AWWWWs and gossip followed. The kids also joined and we were explaining gossip to them as well (errr... well, within their boundaries).

As we were flipping through, I suddenly realised that the photographer had clicked a lot of Soumya's candid 'pichkurs'. Initially I loved the poses but then it hit me. Jealousy took over.

Me: (irate) How many photos did you pose for for this fellow?

There is something about women - they blush when their husbands get jealous. Men panic.

Soumya was beginning to blush when Rishaan answered the question.

Rishaan: (without taking his gaze off the laptop) Many!

When your own son is the one adding fuel to the fire, you reach a point where you don't know if you should focus on the topic of discussion or catch the fuel by its collar. In this moment, I decided to catch the fuel by the collar and discard him out of the scene.

Shakti/Massak

Soumya was sitting down with Anaira and was talking to her. Anaira was telling her about the happenings at her school when Soumya suddenly remembered it was time for some revision of studies. She has been teaching Anaira body parts for a while now. She decided to use the time for revision rather than let Anaira do what she was doing.

She raised Anaira's hands halfway in the air and looked at her.

Soumya: What is this?

Anaira: (manly voice) Shakti!

Soumya laughed it out and thought she will change the gesture. She gently rubbed Anaira's little hands and again asked the question.

Soumya: What is this?

Anaira: Massak!

In case you were wondering, the word is 'massage'. Post this the revision was cancelled.

I Anaira!

As we were playing, Anaira came running over to me shouting 'shu shu, shu shu'. So I immediately carried her like a baby in my outstretched arms and headed toward the bathroom, legs first.

As we approached the bathroom with lightning speed, Anaira kicked the door open firmly. As the door hit hard against the wall and retracted back, I asked her with a look of surprise in my voice and expression.

Me: Aey that door would have broken no doll? Are you Daya? (Daya is a character in the series 'CID' famous for breaking doors open)

Anaira: (sheepishly) No, I Anaila.

I kissed her soft cheeks as I placed her on the seat laughing with despair

See that diaper!

When your kid provides right answers to questions that you assumed were difficult, you feel a bliss like no other. I am sometimes, left with an awe expression not knowing how to react when they answer right.

With Anaira in my hands, I was showing her the various photo frames at my in-laws house and was asking her to identify the person. She was bang on everytime. And then we came to this one frame where Anaira was a four month old baby.

Me: Anaira, do you know who this is?

Anaira: Anaila!

Me: (totally suprised): Wow, how did you know that Anaira?

Anaira: (unfolds the top layer of her pant) See diaper same.

The logic left me speechless. I looked at her pretty little face beaming with pride as she knew she was right.

It is not medicine!

Sometimes kids leave you amazed at the amount of knowledge that they actually have versus how much you believed them to have. Personally, I have reached a point where I have relinquished the need to be amazed at the amount of knowledge surprises I am in for, from the kids.

After a long tiring day and a lovely yummy plate of the famous Belgaum's Niyaaz biryani, I felt like having something to drink. Hence we opened a shining new bottle of Sula's Cabernet Shiraz.

As I carried the wine glass to the hall, Anaira followed me like the rat following the 'Pied Piper'. She quietly walked up to Soumya as I settled in my favourite chair at the dining table and trying her luck, asked if she could get a sip of the juice in Dada's hand. She complimented the request with an expression mighty enough to get a terrorist to surrender as well.

Soumya told her that the drink was medicine and Dada needed to have some so he could feel better after a tiring day. Anaira crumpled the skin on her forehead and made a face:

Anaira: That is not medicine. That is wine!

Soumya looked at me astonished and all I did in return to match the expression was to raise an eyebrow!

Raining cats and dogs!

The Paes family loves going on trips and seeing new places. We love creating new memories and years later, when equations change and newer people enter the family, Soumya and I would love to sit down and browse through these memoirs.

We had been to the heritage sites of Badami-Aihole-Pattadakal and had a lovely time appreciating the ancient architecture. The kids simply enjoyed scampering around the whole open spaces and looking at the architecture as well. However, the scene changed whilst on our way back.

We were driving on the Raichur-Belgaum road when it began pouring very heavily. I must say I have never seen such heavy rainfall as the visibility on the road had come down to literally zero. I had to slow down the SUV to a speed below twenty. All of us were tensed and there was silence in the car in spite of Rishaan and Anaira being present and awake.

My father-in-law seated behind with Rishaan looked at the rain and exclaimed, 'My Gosh, it is pouring cats and dogs'. I was about to say that I differ; this should be elephants when Rishaan sat up and looked outside curiously.

Rishaan: Where are cats and dogs falling? (looking around) Nothing is there!

Kids are fearless. They do not see potential dangers as fear triggers. It is adults that place our understanding of fear into them. The tensed moment was turned into a brief moment of laughter before coming back to square one.

Hot!

Just when we were stepping out, I noticed that Rishaan had taken off his jacket. Without hesitation, I began yelling out asking the reason why he had removed the jacket when it was so cold outside. My angry expression made him fall silent and look to the ground.

Soumya called out from inside clarifying that he had checked with her if he could remove the jacket as he was feeling hot. Immediately realising my folly, I made a puppy face and cajoled Rishaan to come closer to me. He slowly covered the distance and then I started a life lesson for him.

Me: Rishaan, just because someone is shouting at you, you don't have to get scared. You should look them in the eye and reason out with them justifying why you did what you did.

He appeared to listen to me patiently. I continued.

Me: And if you justify and show them the logic, they will feel.... (and I paused, trying to get the right word and whilst I was paused, Rishaan blurted out)

Rishaan: Hot?

Kids are innocent beyond explanation. Not sure if my life lesson was learnt but we had a good laugh.

Bike : Biker :: Car : ?

Rishaan was in the car with us sitting in the back seat talking to us about a lot of stories in his school when a biker just swooshed by overtaking us at an incredible speed. I took the opportunity to deliver a life lesson

Me: Rishaan that biker went so fast! Is it nice to ride so fast?
Rishaan: No Dada (purses his lips disapprovingly)

Delighted, I was about to deliver the life lesson based on his response when a car swooshed by at an equally incredible speed.

Rishaan: Look at that 'carker' Dada. Not nice to go so fast!

The life lesson was parked aside for the day and we all laughed at a puzzled little Rishaan.

Which lift?

The Paes family had been out to meet a family friend at their gated enclave. We got inside the lift after the meeting with our host and as the lift tugged along smoothly to lower floors, the machine stopped at a certain floor. The door opened to reveal the presence of a five year old all by himself. He was trying to search for his family whose exact location he was not sure of.

So all of us in the lift started asking questions out of concern – 'Who you looking for? Which floor? Names? Flat no? ....' He was unable to answer any of them correctly.

When we were thinking of what other questions we could ask and the lift was silent, a concerned Rishaan took the little boy's hand in his and asked:

'Which lift?'

The boy stared back at Rishaan as blank as he was when asked questions by us. We reached the ground floor and Rishaan's concerned eyes kept following the boy till he was reunited with his kin.

Grandmother

Anaira is a star when she dances because she dances like she doesn't care. She dances for herself and for her own enjoyment. And like all Indian parents, we make her dance when we have guests at home.

This one particular time, Anaira was asked to dance as an aunt of mine had come home with her husband. After dancing, she bowed down gracefully whilst the little audience cheered on with claps and admiration. Once the claps slowed down, Anaira walked up to Soumya and started talking to her. She was talking with a very expressive face and spoke non-stop.

After listening to her for about five minutes, Soumya stopped her and exclaimed, 'Anaira, you are one grandmother only.'

Anaira being Anaira, did not waste a single second. She immediately retorted, 'I am Anaira. Grandmother is here.'

She was pointing out to my aunt.

Mamma, Go there!

We all were spending a lazy Saturday morning whilst watching songs on Zoom, Anaira's favourite TV channel! Rishaan was right behind Soumya practicing phonic sounds on one of the apps on my phone.

Soumya turned to me and asked if I could get her phone from the bedroom. I got up and began the search operations but when the operations did not produce any results, I looked at Rishaan and without thinking if he would relate to what I was going to say to him,

Me: Rishaan, can you call Mamma? (meaning that he should call Mamma's phone from my phone)

Rishaan did not waste a minute. He looked at my pretty wife.

Rishaan: Mamma, Go there near Dada!

Communication in the adult's world is so different from communication in the little kiddy world. Only kids can help us realise simplicity!

Mama Paes

As we enjoyed the Independence day holiday with all due regard and gratitude to our freedom fighters, Soumya decided to use this opportunity to check with Rishaan on his self-knowledge levels.

Soumya: What is your name?

Rishaan: Rishaan Paes

Soumya: Very good. What is your sister's name?

Rishaan: Anaira Paes

Soumya: Nice. What is your Mamma's name?

Rishaan: Mamma Paes

By those standards, you'd know what is Dada's name.

Dada has no hair

Whilst we were all discussing on certain personal family matters, Rishaan called someone in the family by another name. So I discussed and tried to make him understand that we cannot rechristen anyone and that we should address them by the name that they already have. But Rishaan did not seem to get the point. And then I had an idea!

Me: Starting today, I will call you 'Satyappa' and not Rishaan.

Rishaan: No, you Satyappa. (Paused and after a while) You Katappa!

Soumya: Errr.... Why Katappa? (Controlling her laughter as she knew where this was headed)

Rishaan: Because Dada has no hair.

Sometimes, life throws you into situations that make you feel like you should smile and cry at the same time.

Bull dog....

On separate occasions, Rishaan has learnt about the existence of a bull. And that there is a breed of dogs that are called bull dogs. Language is sometimes so confusing for the little brains, eh?

We finally arrived at the 'confusion to be put to test' day! One of the traditional godmen came to the house in front of our apartment with a bull that was attired accordingly and played the loud shehnai. The sound got both the Paes' kids out to the balcony. The conversation followed between the two legends:

Rishaan: Do you know that animal with that uncle?

Anaira: No Lishaan. What animal that is?

Rishaan (proudly): That is a bull dog cow.

Anaira: Oh wow!

For a moment, I felt like I saw the bull turn toward Rishaan and look down and shake his head in disgust.

Dlinking water!

So this morning, when Rishaan woke up, he was being shouted at for drinking less water. To avoid more yelling, he took the sipper and started drinking water.

Anaira woke up as well and adjusted herself in Soumya's lap to listen to the whole fiasco. Very aptly, she placed her little palm under her chin and rested her elbow on her leg, thus adjusting her expression and body language to the tense situation.

I winked at my wife to look at her. Soumya looked at her and started explaining to her.

Soumya: See this fellow, Anaira. He does not drink water at all. The whole of Sunday he has not drunk water. This is not acceptable, correct?

Anaira continued to sway her head in disgust throughout. Rishaan fearing the worst of consequences, continued to gulp down the water.

Soumya: You need to advise him, Anaira. What is he doing, hah? What is he doing?

At this question, Anaira looks up and at the peak of her innocence points out,

Anaira: He's dlinking water no!

Burn with fire

Anaira had just scratched Rishaan's face; on his cheeks to be precise. So he came along to complain to me. Our conversation as follows:

Rishaan: See Dada, what that bad girl did to me!

Me: My gosh, Rishaan. This is bad. Is it paining?

Rishaan: Yes Dada.

Me: Should I put some medicine on it?

Rishaan: Yes

Me: But it will burn. Will it be ok?

Rishaan: (after a quick brief moment) Burn with fire?

There are certain things in our life that we have taken for granted with our everyday vocabulary. It takes a little kid with ample innocence to help you understand these differences.

Go out and talk

Sunday night is when we want to sleep really early so that we wake up fresh and early on a Monday morning. However, the kids as usual were all hyperactive and rolling around on the bed telling each other stories.

After a while, Soumya lost it real bad and shouted out aloud, 'Anyone who talks another word is going out of this room!'

Rishaan in all of his pure innocence and very spontaneously, blurts out, 'Go out and talk?'

It took him a spank on his bum to realise how wrong he was. The end of the next minute saw him in deep sleep. Soumya and I continued to be in splits.

She talking to me now!

Rishaan had just gone off to sleep on a normal week night; he had his own tensions of waking up early the next morning. My pretty wife and I were sharing sweet nothings whilst Anaira was rolling on the bed being her mischievous self and trying hard to put herself to sleep. She usually would not go to sleep till Soumya and I slept.

She suddenly rolled up to Soumya, and started talking to her, sensing lack of attention. So I interrupted.

Me: Anaira, you cannot disturb when Mama and Dada are talking.

Anaira: Aey, sshhhh! She talking to me.

Technically, she was right. Hence I decided to shut up.

Customer in the shop

So Rishaan and Anaira play this game called 'shop shop'. Soumya and I need to act as customers and go to the shop so that the 'shopkeepers' can cater to their customers' needs. So that day, both us were busy and hence Rishaan decided that Anaira would be the customer.

Unaware of the change of responsibility, Anaira was still inside the shop (behind the coffee table, customers are supposed to come in the front of the table).

Rishaan (irritated): Get out of my shop!

Me (in the midst of folding clothes): Rishaan, is that the right way to talk?

Rishaan (super mellows down and in a much softer tone): Please get out of my shop!

Anaira seemed totally unaffected and continued to sit snobbishly in the shop whilst her business partner started pondering on his alternatives and options.

With hand!

Kids have an amazing sense of logic which is difficult to argue with. Its just a matter of a perspective shift and suddenly, you see the point; like a 'Eureka' moment!

One morning, I was having Monday morning blues (not sure if it was a Monday) but I simply wanted to stay back home. And when I looked at Anaira lazing around on the sofa, the feeling just got even more intense.

Me: Anaira, I'll go to office?

Anaira: (practically) Ha, go Dada!

Me: Anaira, I no feeling like going to office.

Anaira: (again practically) Don't go Dada (looking at my expression of depression, she chose to give me a hug)

Me: Good.... But Anaira, how to make money then?

Anaira: Don't want money Dada.

Me: But then Anaira, how do we eat food then?

Anaira: (looking at me with a how-can-you-be-so-dumb look) With hand no?

I turned to look at my hand which was travelling at a speed of 60 kms / hr to reach my forehead. Slap!

Forever-Stomach-Full

"Don't eat anything your great-great-grandmother wouldn't recognize as food. There are a great many food-like items in the supermarket your ancestors wouldn't recognize as food. Stay away from these."

—Michael Pollan

Lick the glass!

If there is one utterly distant dream that almost every parent dreams, it would be to sit down on the sofa feeling absolutely relaxed as they'd watch their offspring drink the glass of milk without any fuss and in a manner that will cause absolutely no stress. After a series of moments of pleading, requesting and convincing, I would generally decide to take matters into my own hands; 'matters' in this context is the milk glass to feed baby Anaira.

So this one day, I was feeding Anaira her portion of milk from the glass when three drops of milk overflowed out of the side of the glass. Just so that it does not further trickle down to the ground and create a mess, I asked Anaira to lick the drop off the glass.

Me: Anaira, lick this drop of milk on the side of the glass.

Anaira: (making a face) Chheee no! You lick!

Me: (with an intent to demonstrate, I pulled out my tongue like Katrina Kaif in the Mango drink commercial and began navigating my tongue in the direction of the droplet. Once done, I looked at Anaira confidently) See it's that simple!

Anaira: (again making an expression of disgust) You are dog or what?

There are many times when you feel like a dog due to the various situations life puts you in. This was one of them. When I opened my mouth to come back on her statement, I actually felt I was barking!

Killing flies!

The topic of food brings in a lot of anxiety into the inmates at the Paes' residence. The adults and the kids are left stressed out after the mammoth task of feeding the food. Its like a little battle won once the plate is empty.

It was a rosy crisp morning Sun that overlooked the little apartment whilst the babies were served some delicious breakfast. As they continued to sit at the dining table, Anaira seemed to be distracted (as usual actually). She got down from the dining table and appeared to be searching for something in the air. Rishaan saw my eyes intently following the little explorer and quickly cleared the 'air' for me.

Rishaan: Dada, she is killing flies!

Me: Anaira, how can you kill flies while having breakfast?

She slowly turned in my direction and clapped her hands close to my leg!

With her mouth still full from the last morsel, she looked at me and gave me one of those flashy smiles and said, 'Like this!'

That is for Lishaan!

One of Rishaan's school teachers passes by our apartment sharp at 7.50 AM every day in the school van. It is a mandatory ritual for all of us to wait for her in the balcony because Rishaan is very fond of her. This proves to be highly profitable for us as fifty percent of the breakfast is consumed in less than twenty percent of the time in this period. A lot of hands on parents would love those numbers.

I was feeding Anaira and she was creating a fuss. So as we were waiting, like all normal Indian parents, I made use of an opportunity when Anaira was distracted.

Me: (swiftly bringing the morsel of breakfast close to her mouth) See see, Shankari Ma'am came! (Anaira falls for the bait)

Anaira: (disapprovingly) She comes for Lishaan, not for me!

I twisted my lips and turned a deaf ear. I was one morsel down anyways! Later in the day, apparently, while she was at school, she was quoted requesting her own teacher to start visiting our apartment like Rishaan's teacher.

Senses!

Ever since I got home a few science books, I think I have been learning more than the kids. Like I never knew that the octopus had three hearts. I half knew that Pluto was termed as a dwarf planet. So much to learn!

Anyways, this one morning, we were learning about mammals. And the fact that mammals are animals that give birth and don't lay eggs. Calling it out as I am sure I would have enlightened someone amongst the readers. One of the characteristics about mammals is the fact that they have the five senses. So I closed the book and spoke to Rishaan.

Me: So you know what are senses?

Rishaan: No!

Me: Hmmmm. Your eyes; what do they do?

Rishaan: They look!

Me: Your nose?

Rishaan: It smells!

Me: Your ears?

Rishaan: They can listen.

Me: Your tongue?

Rishaan: It licks!

Me: (laughing) It tastes. And your fingers?

Rishaan: To play the piano!

Kids can be so creative if we only let them explore and think. I have never stopped being amazed at this quality of a child.

Chest is also filled!

When kids have to come up with excuses on not doing something, even the wisest of men raise their hands in despair. They throw in such bouncers and googlies that we are amazed at the level of thinking that they have. In the bargain, we forget to answer.

One lovely evening, Rishaan was throwing tantrums for eating his dinner. I was pushing him to finish his food fast. He kept lingering over the food and buying time. After a while of me stuffing food inside his little mouth, he exploded.

Rishaan: My stomach was full. Now my chest is also getting full.

As a parent, tell me what am I supposed to say back when confronted with a situation like this?

Respect food!

With the years of experience that I have had in bringing up the two pranksters at home, I think I am qualified enough to say that every second parent in this world has the dream that one day, their offspring would obediently walk up to the kitchen, serve themselves food in a plate and lick the plate clean before the wink of an eye or at least without wasting time.

Since the time Rishaan and Anaira were born, Soumya and I would have spent at least two thirds of our life with our hands dipped in food. And just when we would finish with one and walk up to wash our hands, it would be time to start feeding the other. You can imagine the relief we have had since the time, we started getting the kids to eat their own food.

So this one day, Anaira was throwing tantrums for eating food. She was playing with the food that was served to her and was wasting time much to my disgust. After a while, I thundered.

Me: ANAIRA THAT IS NOT THE WAY! Please show the food some respect!

Before I could blink my big eyes, Anaira closed her eyes and joined her little hands in reverence facing in the direction of the plate.

My thundering turned into a thunderous laughter.

Cancel!

A lavish lunch was served for all of us (courtesy the lovely Mrs Paes) and at the outset, I had declared that each of us was responsible for finishing the food. No one was supposed to be fed; all of this with an intent to be able to enjoy the lazy Sunday afternoon.

As expected, Anaira was the first one to stop eating; to add to my temper she started dancing. I decided to act.

I made an imaginary call to the North Pole to Santa and detailed out aloud to him about the current situation and also being amazed at the fact that he already knew a lot of details owing to the invisible CCTV camera that he had installed in our house ahead of Christmas. Every time, the conversation went in the direction of cancelling the gift, Anaira would quickly gulp in a morsel. I promised to call back Santa and give him an update in case the situation turned hostile again. Four calls later, the conversation was something like this:

Me: Yeah hi santa!.... Oh you saw her stopping food again..... Yeah... Yeah....

Anaira: (turns to me and taps on my shoulder) Cancel gift!

Guess I needed to know when a certain weapon expires. This one backfired.

He is not hot!

On a lazy Sunday morning, I was given the mammoth task of ensuring that both the babies finish their breakfast!

I decided to take up the challenge. However, I realized pretty soon that this was going to be more than a challenge and hence it is going to take more than just the routine to ensure that the task was completed.

Rishaan: Ouch! This bread omlette is hot! I can't eat this right now.

Me: (coming up with a strategy) That should not matter, Rishaan… (increasing the intensity in my eyes) … because YOU are hotter! Come on now, lets show the bread who is hot!

Anaira: What??!!??

Me: (reiterating) Rishaan is hot, Anaira.

Anaira looked at Rishaan and touched his forehead. Then turns to me with an angry look.

Anaira: Why you telling lies? He is cold! No fever.

Sometimes, the power of manipulation falls flat with the digital kids of these days.

You think in your mind!

It was yet another morning as usual at the Paes residence. Soumya and I were racing with time amidst Rishaan's and Anaira's 'more than occasional' giggles and fights.

While I was in the kids' room getting Rishaan's bag, Soumya and Rishaan had a deal behind my back that he will get a Choco Pie to carry to school. Unaware of the deal and in my hurry to get to school, I swooshed out of the room to appear in the hall and started opening the main door.

Rishaan: Wait, wait! mamma is giving me Choco Pie.

Me: (as if stopped from launching ISRO's Mangalyaan at the last milli second) Why would you want Choco Pie now?

Rishaan: (slapping his forehead with his palm and with a God like face; thoughtfully spoke) I didn't want. Mamma forced me.

His smile was the smile of the Mona Lisa.

Lunch box

Rishaan had been a very good boy as per Soumya's standards. He had eaten all of his food except for the two last morsels. The struggle was on for the last two morsels to be finished.

After the struggle for the Indian independence, this struggle between a mother and a child to gulp down the last few morsels stands second.

Post a lot of persuasion, right when Soumya felt she had over powered him and that morsel was going to disappear, Rishaan spoke unexpectedly.

Rishaan: I am lunch box or what?

Soumya: (shocked out of her wits) What?

Rishaan: (throwing his little hands in the air) You are filling me like a lunch box!

The connotations that kids use sometimes can make a mother feel more guilty than victorious.

Go madu beda!

Rishaan was eating his breakfast by himself and he was dreaming away instead of munching. My blood pressure continued to rise above sea level in a futile attempt to fasten up his process of completion of the breakfast.

Looking at my helpless pleading falling on deaf ears, our maid pitched in.

Maid: (in Kannada) Who wants to come to Amod's house? (Amod is Rishaan's best apartment friend)

Rishaan: (in English) I will come, Aunty.

Saying this, he started hogging on his breakfast. In the next two mins, he was back to square one. So I put some kerosene to the fire.

Me: Rishaan, aunty has finished her work and she will go now to Amod's house.

Rishaan: (in his broken Kannada) Aunty, 'go' madu beda! (Don't go!)

For those of you who understand the language, you will find it funny. For the rest, do consult with Rishaan and he will explain the meaning of the sentence he created.

Relish!

Rishaan was creating a fuss to eat. So I advised him

Me: Rishaan, don't make a fuss to eat. In fact you should not eat, you should relish the food.

Rishaan: What is relish?

Soumya was eating the new Amul Venezuela Ebony Twist (55% dark). So I suggested that she show Rishaan what it means to relish. Soumya being Soumya, created expressions that exaggerated the art of relishing. I turned to Rishaan.

Me: So Rishaan, to relish means.....

Rishaan (interrupting): To eat like a cow!

I turned to look at the cow... errrrr.... Soumya who was staring back at Rishaan, trying to figure out which part of her expression made him think about a cow.

I don't eat sticks!

Somehow, my generation was fortunate enough to be able to enjoy the sheer pleasure of digging our teeth into freshly 'robbed' sugarcane from fields nearby. Those are priceless moments that the generations of today will rarely get to witness with all the chaos and the 'discipline' that has come their way. As parents, Soumya and I have been far too careful about what kids consume. But alas!

As we were walking down the stairs of the apartment, we bumped into one of our neighbours. They were carrying sugarcane for the household; maybe some religious purpose. Rishaan had not seen sugarcane till then.

Rishaan: (smiling) Hello!

Neighbour: Hi Rishaan. You want to eat this (pointing to the sugarcane in his hand)

Rishaan looked at the cane disapprovingly for the next five seconds and then spoke.

Rishaan: No uncle, I don't eat sticks.

The neighbor and I exchanged embarrassed looks and closing greetings. It took me futile attempts to explain to Rishaan that what he saw was the raw material for sugar. Not until the following weekend that I bought some sugarcane and demonstrated to the kids about how do we eat the delicacy, did Rishaan try out the experience.

Who is Bahubali?

Most kids and food are like parallel lines with no sight of meeting each other. But as parents, we may give up on a lot of other things in life but feeding our kids and ensuring that they have eaten is something that we will never give up.

On a separate note, Rishaan is a huge fan of the movie character 'Bahubali'. In fact, some of the kids in the apartment actually thought that his name is Bahubali because he had introduced himself as Bahubali to them.

The other day, I was feeding Anaira her glass of milk and she was throwing tantrums. So I thought of using some of the motivational speaker speeches.

Me: ANAIRAAAAA, this milk is getting scared of you (shaking the milk glass). See, it is getting scared and shaking. It is saying, 'I don't want Anaira to drink me. Brrrrr.....'

Anaira continued to stare at my bizarre personality change. I ignored and continued.

Me: ANAIRAAAAA, show this milk who is Bahubali. WHO IS BAHUBALI, TELL ANAIRA, WHO IS BAHUBALI?

Anaira (very calmly, shrugging her shoulders): Rishaan.

Answering Back

"Do not teach your children never to be angry; teach them how to be angry"

—Lyman Abbott

Slow bike!

Rishaan and Anaira love bike rides to school and in fact they prefer the bike over the car as they love the breeze in their face. Anaira sits in the front and Rishaan sits behind me. Unfortunately for them however, I am a very slow and careful rider. To add to it, that day, we began having a conversation on the bike as we inched our way to school even though we were late as usual. Rishaan innocently started a new topic.

Rishaan: Dada, when Mamma takes us to school, she races all the other bikes.

Me: WHAT? I had told Mamma to go slow when she is with you guys on the bike.

Rishaan: (realising he was in deep sh** and in an attempt to save the 'first' love of his life) No. Actually, all these other bikes go very slow!

Me: Wait, I will go and shout at Mamma today.

Anaira: Aey you chup le! Go little fast!

There are very few topics on which you can argue with Anaira. I am yet to discover them.

Chup le!

The recent eclipse had created quite a bit of excitement at the Paes' residence. The kids were pretty gung ho about the fact that the moon would first appear full and then a part of it would disappear and then appear again. Since the time they were born, this was anyways their first eclipse at least in their conscious state.

So, once back home from office, I joined the kids as we lay down in the bedroom munching on some grub, trying to take a good look at the eclipsed moon. Soumya was trying to take pictures of the moon. The kids were rolling over each other to get a good glimpse of the moon.

In all of that excitement, the fatherly instinct within me realised that Anaira had got on the bed with her chappals.

Me: (being very sweet in an attempt to not spoil the moment) Doll, are you supposed to wear chappals whilst on the bed?

Anaira: Chup le! You see the moon!

Like I said, there are indeed very few topics in this world on which you can argue with Anaira.

I touched my plate!

Anaira was banished from the dining table as she had not even touched the plate of delicious noodles. She angrily perched herself on the sofa and after a discussion, she apologized and asked that she be given her plate once again. After a lot of persuasion and thought, we agreed.

But then like they say, 'History Repeats!' Once again, she did not eat. I began nagging her that she was not 'touching' her plate at all. Unconsciously, I repeated the word 'touching the plate' about 3 times at least. This time I had lost it.

Me: ANAIRA, THAT IS IT! I am going to take the plate away now (saying this I got up in aggression)

Anaira: (immediately touching the plate) I touched my plate!

I stopped mid-way. The moment froze. I was caught up in the *'chakravyuh'* of my own words.

Read your book!

On a happy Friday morning, I was devouring the very interesting read 'The Pin Drop pinciple' when Rishaan woke up. We exchanged morning wishes with each other and he settled next to me with his toy cars. I decided to read out aloud so that Rishaan also can hear. I continued reading till I hit the word 'attitude'.

Rishaan: Attitude? What is attitude?

Me: (Closing the book and getting ready for a long conversation) Hmmm! Attitude.... Let's put it this way! There is good attitude and bad attitude.

Rishaan: (repeating the sentence and giving out the right verbal nods)

Me: Yesterday, Anaira was angry with us and was slouching on the sofa. That was bad attitude. But when mamma asked you drink your milk yesterday, you willingly took the glass and drank. That was good attitude.

There are more aspects.... Blah.... Blah... Blah.....

Rishaan: (cutting me short) You read your book!

Me: You want to listen more?

Rishaan: No you read slowly to yourself!

In the last decade of my training experience, this was the first trainee who was so direct in my face.

Don't give advice!

As a responsible father, I have always believed that I should advise my kids even if they don't understand or if the advice is too much for their age.

Today as I was giving Rishaan his bath, I poured some normal hot water on him and he yelled as it was the temperature of the sun. After I had cooled down the water and Rishaan as well, I decided to advise him irrespective of his response to it.

Me: Rishaan can I give you some golden advice for life?

Rishaan: No

Me: (I still continued) Don't over react in life no matter what.

Rishaan: (mockingly) Why?

Me: Try to stay calm always

Rishaan: Chheee.

Me: Because when we get excited, we sometimes tend to behave stupidly. So did you understand the golden advice?

Rishaan: Yes

Me: And what is it?

Rishaan: Don't give advice!

My eyes popped out and if it popped out anymore, my eyeball would have been left hanging out.

Love for School

"Children want the same things we want. To laugh, to be challenged, to be entertained and delighted."

—Dr Seuss

Interview – Part 1

How we wish we were kids for life. As kids we could just be bluntly honest in someone's face and at the same time not even worry about consequences. As adults, how many times have we had to swallow our words just because we could not honestly speak our heart and mind out.

Anyways, Anaira's school admission interview was around the corner. The school was decided as we had done enough and more research during Rishaan's time and without doubt, it would be the same school for obvious and convenience reasons. We just had to make sure that Anaira cracks the interview. The rest of it, owing to the political influence of Rishaan would be a cakewalk.

So Soumya had been continuously preparing her for the same by conducting mock interviews.

Soumya: Hello

Anaira: Hello

Soumya: What is your name?

Anaira: Anaila

Soumya: What is your father's name?

Anaira: Dada.

Soumya: What is Dada's name?

Anaira: Loysen.

Soumya: What is Mamma's name?

Anaira: Shomya

Soumya: Very good.

Me: Would you like to study in our school?

Anaira: No. I only want to watch Motu Patlu.

Though we want our kids to be honest, somewhere honesty in itself is a contradiction. It has its limitations. Anaira was just being brutally honest; when life is already so beautiful, why change; why school?

Interview – Part 2

Soumya had spent a good amount of time that afternoon grilling Anaira and throwing in different types of questions at her. For a moment, it felt like Anaira was attending the IAS mock interviews but then sometimes, preparing in life for something tougher than what you are aiming at makes sense.

After a while when Soumya walked into the kitchen to look at the 'halwa' that was cooking, I took over.

Me: Anaira, I will be the ma'am ok now? I will take your interview.

Anaira: Ok.

Me: Hello Anaira.

Anaira: Hello Ma'am.

Me: What is your name?

Anaira: Anaila. Just now, you only told no.

Tumhara naam kya hai Basanti wala situation took place in my house that day courtesy Anaira!

Interview – Part 3

The mock interviews were continuing at home with incredible zeal. The objective was getting clearer and clearer to Anaira that she needed to crack this bad if she needed to be studying along with Rishaan in the same school. Somehow, I knew that the elder brother's reputation would make it a cakewalk for the little lady to have a red carpet welcome in the school.

Secretly, I had started enjoying these mock interviews with little Anaira.

Me: Anaira, you should always respond when Ma'am speaks with you.

Anaira: Ok Dada.

Me: Hello Anaira.

Anaira: (raises her eyebrows with a question mark) What Ma'am?

It definitely would take a very hard hearted person or a person without a heart to not provide Anaira admission to their school. Fingers crossed!

Interview – Part 4

So on the D day, the Paes' arrived! Needless to say, late for the interview. Anaira had rehearsed enough such that she could contest state elections.

While waiting outside the Principal's office, I decided to role play her one last time.

Me: Let's do it one last time, Anaira.

Anaira: (in a super good girl Avatar) Ok Dada.

Me: Hello Anaira!

Anaira: Hello Ma'am! (And then she continued in a very excited tone) And then ma'am will say, 'Wow! What a pletty girl! So bootiful dress! So nice lipistick!'

Poor girl! I decided to not have any more mocks with her. It had got to her head. As I looked at her, she was waving at and wishing every one - the gardener, the ayya not knowing who was the 'One' she had to impress. She was out on a mission to impress everyone who would walk the insides of the school compound that day.

Interview – Part 5

So we were finally done with the much awaited interview. Anaira came out with flying colours. She was super cool inside the cabin and at certain times did speak out of turn like saying that she teased the domestic help in the morning and stuff. It was all laughed at.

We then proceeded to the office to complete the rest of the formalities. As I was filling up the forms and writing the cheques, the office staff were trying to get Anaira's attention. Anaira however was more than done for the day and hence chose to ignore everyone.

Me: (continuing to write and not looking up) Anaira, say hi or else they will cancel your admission.

Anaira: (dramatically looking up from what she was doing and brightening up her face as she pulled her head up) Ah! Hiiiiieeee!

The office staff ROFLed at her theatrical display of expression.

Socks Misunderstanding!

Soumya was getting Rishaan ready to go to school while Anaira looked on. I was in the bedroom getting myself to look presentable at yet another day at work. Whilst I threw in some moisturizer on my face, Soumya called out with a tone that subtly announced 'work' coming my way.

Soumya: On your way back, get socks for the kids.

Me: (In disbelief) Socks?

Let's take a moment and understand the context of the wife and the context as understood by the husband. I understood the sentence as, 'while on the way back after dropping the kids to school, I need to pick up new pair of socks from the shop'. This was ridiculous as I had to rush to office after that.

On the other hand, however, Soumya meant that on the way out of the bedroom, I should pick up the kids socks from the cupboard. Now you may read the conversation once again and then continue.

The conversation continued in the same ridiculous way for a while.

Soumya: Ya re. Socks for the kids!

Me: (walking out of the bedroom and doing the action of wearing invisible socks) I should get socks?

Soumya: (confused) Yes re socks! Why?

Rishaan: (walking from underneath Soumya's nose half clothed) Ayyoyo! Wait I'll only get!

As he walked past me, he looked at me as if I was ridiculously useless in this house and could not get any work done! Coincidentally, my wife thinks the same about me. Sounds familiar, eh?

Choco Pie

Rishaan has always been a huge fan of Choco Pie and it was getting into an addiction. We were contemplating ways of getting him off the 'substance'. One day when Soumya went to pick him up, his teacher called her in and advised that Rishaan was getting obsessed with the sweet and that we needed to curb the same. Rishaan was close and listening, so she also added that it was not good for health.

The next day, the following conversation took place!

Soumya: Rishaan, can I give you Chocos?

Rishaan: (out of concern) Just call Ma'am and check with her if it is good for health.

Soumya: (shocked) Why re? It is ok for you to eat!

Rishaan: You didn't know about Choco Pie also. Just call her and check.

One of the many times in parenthood when you feel utterly useless as a parent!

School?

Recently when we had gone down to the play area in the apartment, Rishaan did something that he was not supposed to do. I first wanted him to realise what he had done but he did not seem to get the point. He was still giggling away.

Giving up, I decided to announce the punishment and that is that he would not get to come down in the evening to the play area for the whole of next week.

Me: Rishaan for the whole of next week, you will sit at home and not do anything.

Rishaan: School?

I don't know if he was asking the question to clarify or with hopes in his head, but nonetheless his spontaneity amazed me.

Fan

It is amazing how kids can relate to anything in its simplest form. When you speak to a child about something, most of the times, if not all, the image that they have about the 'something' is entirely different from the image that you have in your mind. That's how beautifully innocent kids are.

We had just come back from an extravagant display of performance by all the school kids of Rishaan's school. The little man also had put up a brilliant performance along with his classmates to bring out the harvesting season of Punjab. It was a very catchy number that was used and in addition to the kids, some of the parents also shook a leg; Punjabi music after all.

So dressed like a handsome Punjabi munda, he had enthralled the audience whilst on the stage with his dance partner. When he came back home, I spoke to him about the performance.

Me: Rishaan, you were amazing on the stage. I have now become your fan.

Rishaan: (puzzled for a brief moment) Then you will also now start going round and round?

For a moment, I actually felt my mind going round and round.

Goats!

This happened at a time when Anaira had not yet started going to school. After dropping Rishaan to school, Anaira enjoys the ride back home, especially the breeze on her face. On the way, we pass a temple area where a few goats are tied throughout the day. She has accepted them as her goat friends whom she waves out to, every day. The goats are absolutely clueless of the existence of their waving friend.

One day, I was getting late to office and hence I raced past the goats allowing her no time to wave out. So she lost her cool and began arguing with me on the rest of the way.

Anaira: Dada, why you didn't stop for my goat friends?

Me: Sorry sorry, Anaira! I'm getting late to office no.

Anaira: No but you should have stopped. I didn't say bye to them only.

Me: (sarcastically) They are your friends or what?

Anaira: Yeah

Me: And what are their names?

Anaira: (pauses for a second and then lets it out) Goats!

I decided to focus on reaching office on time.

Fairy Tales

*"I will defend the importance of bed time stories
to my last gasp."*

—J. K. Rowling

What's in a lanmdp!

What I love about kids and something that I teach in my training classes, is that kids speak their heart out! When a thought comes to a child's creatively genius brain, they do not let it escape and speak their heart out or ask questions.

A couple of days back, Soumya had narrated out the story of Alladin and the lamp and the kids had loved it! A few mornings later while munching on breakfast, Rishaan spoke with his mouth full of the dosa morsel.

Rishaan: Mamma, whatff comesh oud of the lanmdp?

Soumya: What?

Rishaan: (repeating) Mamma, whattff comesh oud of the lanmdp?

Anaira: Genie!

Soumya looked at Anaira and it took her a while to realize that Rishaan was asking 'What comes out of the lamp?' in connection with the recently narrated story, 'Alladin and the lamp'.

This had to be telepathy or some kind of voodoo magic. They had to belong to the same clan to be able to understand each other's language so well, a clan called babies I guess!

Story

I am an advocate of not correcting certain pronunciations of words that our kids use. If not now, then when else will they make mistakes? One of our family friend's kid used to pronounce the cold drink 'Sprite' as 'Saprite' and once when we had been to their place, he explained that they did not want to correct him till a while when he'd start going to school. That concept stayed with me.

Anaira wanted to tell me a story and looking at me sitting on the sofa reading the book 'The Power of Now', she toddled up to me.

Anaira: Dada, I'll tell one stoly?

Me: Ok doll, tell!

Anaira: One this pon time.....

I truly apologize as I did not hear the rest of the sentence or story as my laughter drowned the tiny creative voice.

Siblings

"Siblings: Children of the same parents, each of whom is perfectly normal until they get together."

—Sam Levenson

Self-defense

One fine Sunday morning, I was teaching Rishaan the art of self-defense from whatever limited knowledge I had, but all the action was not yielding any results. However, when I turned around, I noticed Anaira trotting around. How did I not think of this before? I had the 'sakshat' Bruce Lee in the house and I was thinking of ways of teaching self-defense to Rishaan. So I changed my strategy.

Me: Anaira, come here!

Anaira: (comes) Ha Dada!

Me: Now Rishaan look at this. When someone is trying to come to attack you, first hold their hand.

Anaira: (totally getting into the character and enjoying it too, started to attack me with the other hand)

Me: So Rishaan, this is the most obvious thing the person will do - attack with the other hand. So you need to hold the other hand with your other hand. (Held her second hand as well very confidently)

Without a warning, Anaira being Anaira bounced her head on my nose. Wham! After seeing stars for two whole minutes while the kids laughed about what just happened, I decided that this needs to be left to the professionals.

I am now enquiring about karate classes; not for Rishaan but from a very futuristic perspective for Anaira's future husband!

Fellow!

Anaira and Rishaan were fighting in the bedroom whilst Soumya and I were in the kitchen. So these days, we are making conscious efforts to avoid getting involved in their fights unless, you know, it may get criminal.

Anaira came complaining in the kitchen about Rishaan. He had pulled her dress and due to which her body had moved violently. She enacted the scene and said that he had done this to her.

Me: Really Anaira? Please call that fellow here!

Anaira: (calling out in the direction of the bedroom) FELLOW? FELLOW? BAD BOY? DIRTY FELLOW?

Soumya and I stared at each other. I think due to these type of situations, we have started looking at each other more often; nonetheless, our love for each other is constantly on the rise.

You know who he is?

Anaira was beating away Rishaan out of irritation. I saw it once and patiently advised Rishaan not to talk to her for the rest of the day. The second time I warned Anaira that she should not touch my son. The third time I lost it bad.

Me: (going intimidatingly close to her) You beat him once more and you will have to bear the brunt. Do you know who he is? (meaning to say that he was her elder brother and loved her so much but then the question did not go as planned)

Anaira looked at me as if I had had a minor stroke of amnesia. She wrinkled up her forehead and looked at me intensely.

Anaira: He is Lishaan, no?

Intimidatingly close that I was, I suddenly straightened my back. I clearly had not seen that one coming!

Father and daughter

Anaira and I were in a Saturday morning fun mood. We were lying lazy on the couch and finishing the daily dose of hugs. Anaira suddenly stated that she wanted to put on the idiot box. Soumya put off the demand by announcing in the negative to the request.

But then this is Anaira and Anaira does what Anaira does. As Rishaan was sitting on the same couch, she jumped over him, switched on the TV and then jumped back in my refugee camp. Listening to the sound of the TV welcome music, Soumya came out

Soumya: (thundering) Who put on the TV?

Rishaan: (looking up from his books) This father and daughter!

Soumya: Why they don't have work or what?

Rishaan: Uhuh! I asked them. They said no work!

We literally ROFLed.

On the way back!

Everyday, Rishaan gets picked up from school by Soumya and Anaira. As a practice, a harmless investigation takes place on the way back between Soumya and Rishaan. That day, Anaira decided to take the lead as Mamma was busy manoeuvring traffic.

Anaira: How was your day, Lishaan?

Rishaan: I did lot of activities at school. Lot of work was there. I was very busy. What you did at home?

Anaira: I did *colouling* (colouring), watched *Motu Patlu* and ate *mum mum*. You finished your lunch box?

Rishaan: (silence)

Soumya picked the clue and jumped in at the opportunity.

Soumya: (3rd degree tone) You didn't finish your tiffin?

Rishaan rolled his eye to look at Anaira to show her the mess she had created.

Anaira: It's ok, Lishaan. *Leach* home and finish your food.

Rishaan: (smiles) Ok Anaira.

Anaira: He is good boy, mamma.

Siblings are partners-in-crime. For three seconds, Soumya forgot looking at the road and stared at the little mischief makers who by now had covered their mouths and were laughing.

You feeling bad for me?

Rishaan and Anaira had just fought.... as usual. By the time however, that we intervened, Anaira had deftly scratched Rishaan's face thereby causing a deep scratch. All of this because, I had taken off a toy from her due to bad behaviour.

I brought down the roof. Blah, blah! And ultimately, Anaira was crying her lungs out.

After a while of wailing, I decided to make her dole out an apology. I spoke.

Me: Please walk up to Rishaan and apologize. Please talk to him. Ask him if he is feeling bad.

Anaira: (walks up to Rishaan as she is crying) *Solly* Lishaan.

Rishaan: Will you do it again? (and looks at me with one eye)

Me: Anaira, please ask him if he is feeling bad after what you did?

Anaira: (still crying) Are you feeling bad for me?

Innocent as they are, kids ensure that they always take advantage of any vulnerable situation.

I'll handle it!

On an SOS call from Soumya to join her at a place away from home, Rishaan, Anaira and I began running helter skelter with an intent to get ready and scoot out of the home quick.

Whilst Rishaan had smoothly begun the process of getting dressed up, out of the experiences of his life, Anaira was unable to remove her T-shirt and insisted that there was a button behind that needed to be removed.

Me: (slowly losing my temper) Anaira, there is no button. Just pull it off.

Anaira: (crying) Button is there. Lemove button.

Me: (as I continued to decide on the clothes that they'd wear) I am telling you there is no button. Don't irritate me.

Anaira: (crying louder) Button is there. LEMOVE!

Me: (That-was-it condition) It is a dumb simple T-shirt. JUST PULL IT OVER!

Enter Rishaan.

Rishaan: (signalling out to me to keep quiet) Come Anaira. I will remove the button.

He behaves as if an imaginary button was removed.

Anaira: (smiling) Thank you Lishaan.

Rishaan looked at me and smirked. Both the musketeers calmly walked away leaving me feel like a soldier who had just lost a war.

You play with her!

With an urgent assignment at hand, I was fiercely working on my laptop. Anaira was getting bored and began purring around me with an intent to get my attention.

When she realised her attempts were going in vain, she started climbing over my legs. I looked up and with an absolute attempt to not lose my temper, I looked toward Rishaan who was drawing some pictures on a book.

Me: Anaira doll, can you please go and play with Rishaan? I'm slightly held up!

Rishaan: I am also busy re. You play with her no for now.

I looked at him with a jaw hanging down, not ready to believe what I had just heard. I looked at my laptop and then at his book and then at Anaira. She was smiling at me knowing I had no choice.

Sshhh! Sleep quietly!

After having cleared the dishes, Soumya and I decided to sip on some of our favourite wine, Jacob's Creek before ending the day. I poured out the contents of the seven year old into the dazzling lush glasses and we headed to the bedroom where lay the two tired little warriors.

Rishaan was snoring away as we decided to sit down next to the heavenly looking angels. We were, however definitely not prepared for what happened next.

Anaira was sleeping facing Rishaan when she suddenly opened her eyes clearly disturbed from the snoring sound. She looked at him and lifted her hand and did the unthinkable.

She closed his open mouth and then mumbled putting her index finger on her rosy lips.

Anaira: Sshhh! Shleep quietly!

She slept almost immediately post that. Stunned, Soumya and I turned to look at each other for five seconds of silence before bursting out into peels of laughter. We were glad that we had had an opportunity to be a part of that moment. Heaven knows how many such moments do we actually miss!

Let's beat him!

In parental journeys, it is very rare when you find your offspring focused and concentrating on an activity that is anti-noise and is contributing to peace in the house. Research says that you should not disturb them during such moments and let them be as this will help them focus in life and learn concentration as a skill.

For me, the below moment in fact pushed me to be a true believer in this research not for anything else but for my physiological safety. Rub kids on the wrong side and you are in to bear the consequences, especially when there are two of them.

This one morning, Rishaan was sitting quietly and drawing. I got into a mischievous mood and gave him a little 'tapli' on his head. He immediately escalated the physical abuse to the highest authority in the house, Soumya. My gorgeous wife was busy and hence ignored the little man.

I smirked and pulled out my little tongue to tease Rishaan. From somewhere below me and closer to the ground, I heard a little squeaky voice scream, 'Lets beat him, Rishaan.'

It took me three seconds to realise that the mob had decided to take matters into their own hands due to the failure of the judicial mechanism at home.

I was pinned to the floor and the two cute little miscreants were placing tiny non-painful blows on my stomach.

Tattoo

With each passing day in parental journeys, one thing is assured – you cannot stop being surprised at the varied display of activities and knowledge shared by a kid. Sometimes, hilarious and other times in real awe, but the surprises rarely stop.

Anaira walked out of the bedroom and straight to me.

Anaira: Dada, I also want one tattoo.

Me: (surprised) And do you know what is a tattoo?

Anaira: That on the hand, some drawing will be there no. (showing her forearm)

Me: (super surprised) And where did you see a tattoo?

Anaira: On Lishaan's hand!

I walked up to the bedroom and saw the young man totally engrossed into drawing a second tattoo with a pen on his forearm, something that is forbidden in the house. The only surface that a pen should write on is paper.

As Rishaan got one 'tapli' on the back of his head, I was particularly amused to see Anaira cover her mouth and laugh. Not sure if she really wanted a tattoo or this was an innovative complaint.

Rishaan is good boy

Rishaan and Anaira were fighting over a toy phone. Rishaan claimed that he had sighted the phone first. Anaira's claim was that she had touched the phone first.

Unfortunately, as a parent you are stuck in the negotiation of such stupid irrational things that you don't believe that you are actually going to do it. Nonetheless!

Me: Rishaan, come on. Let go of the phone.

Rishaan: No

Me: Anaira, you are my sweet doll no? You give the phone. Let it be.

Anaira: No

A brilliant idea came to my head. Or at least that's what I thought. Confidently, I started.

Me: Who is the good boy / girl here?

Even whilst Rishaan was contemplating the answer,

Anaira: (as quick as light) Rishaan!

When you are very clear with what you want in your head, answers to questions are but a piece of cake.

Rishaan is angry

Rishaan was watching a video on YouTube and I needed the phone to make a call. He did not want to give the phone and hence this led to him getting stubborn and a momentary act of being pissed off with me. As he walked away from the scene, he gave me a stare that was the 'will see you in hell' types.

Anaira walks up to me quietly as if she did not want to be noticed.

Anaira: He is angry. Talk to him.

I was shocked at her words but yet shrugged my shoulders to show that I was not interested.

Whilst I write this joke, I can hear Anaira speak in the bedroom with the angry young man.

Anaira: What happened, Lishaan? Don't wolly. It's ok!

Siblings love is a beautiful phenomenon; when they have to fight, they fight as if there is no tomorrow and when they display love, they display as if they would want yesterday's time back as well.

Patience Dada

I was having Monday morning blues and to add to it, Anaira had somehow caught hold of a crayon and had written on the floor. I totally lost it and went berserk on the poor little thing. But then the little fighter that she was; she put up a fight as always.

I wanted to take away the crayon from her hand but each time I thought I had caught hold of the crayon, she deftly pulled it back, whilst continuing to keep the angry expression on her face. She was angry with me because I had shouted at her.

At this point, Rishaan who has been watching the whole drama unfold between the father and the daughter, decided to come to my rescue. He calmly pats my pant from behind.

Rishaan: (waving a hand to back out) Patience, Dada. (Turns to look at Anaira) Now see ha. This good girl, how she will give the crayon to Dada.

Sure enough, and almost immediately, the 'Good girl' turned around and with a smiling face handed over the crayon to Dada. Rishaan looked at me and gave me one of those smiles that you'd get from a magician whose magic trick just worked like magic.

The balcony door was open, just that I did not make use of the opportunity.

One more for my sister

And a lovely evening at the mall needs to be complimented with a KFC meal. And hence we walked upto the KFC counter and stood in the line. I told Rishaan that I would need his help in placing the order and he agreed with a thumbs up.

As we neared the 'order taker', I lifted Rishaan and placed him on the counter. A tiny tug at my pant indicated I had to get Anaira up as well. Rishaan and I started our conversation with the executive.

Me (into Rishaan's ear): Hello Uncle!

Rishaan: Hello Uncle!

Exec: Hi!

Me: I need a mingles bucket

Rishaan: I need a mingles bucket

Exec: Sure sir. Anything else?

Me: And a Five in one meal box

Rishaan: And a Five in one meal box

Exec: Done. Anything else?

Me: That will be all!

Rishaan: That will be all!

Exec: 5 mins sir.

I guess the executive was impressed with Rishaan and he got him a Choco Pie. Rishaan was overjoyed.

Me: Thank you uncle

Rishaan: Thank you uncle

Exec: You are welcome!

Me: (nothing)

Rishaan: Uncle, Can you give one for my sister also?

The poor executive had not seen this coming. Anaira and the executive exchanged embarrassed looks for the first time.

Baby Language

*"Everything you say to your child is absorbed,
catalogued and remembered."*

—Maria Montessori

Aladdin and the lamp

As soon as I reached home last night, the kids were ready to go to bed. I told Soumya that I will put them to bed and that she can look after the rest of the kitchen chores. So we all slipped into the warm blanket and as was the ritual I began telling them a story - Aladdin and the lamp!

Me: I will tell you a story that has magic in it...... Bla blah blah.... And when the genie asked Aladdin for his wish, Aladdin tried his luck by asking for an ice cream from Corner House. The genie immediately got the ice cream and Aladdin started eating it.

Anaira: No ice cream for Genie?

Rishaan: He would have given him also.

Me: blah blah blah.... He wanted a burger from McD. Blah blah blah... And that is the end of the story

Rishaan: Where was the magic in the story?

I looked at him in amazement. Aladdin and the lamp is all about magic.

It was only later, however that Soumya revealed to me that I had to do a 'thun' sound before the ice cream or the burger appeared or basically magic happened in a story. Only then would he feel it is magic. Poor fellow! The disillusionment kids have about magic!

'Thun'!

Of Course!

Lately, Anaira has taken great liking for the phrase 'Of Course!' The below instances display the passion she showed for the use of this phrase. I must say that I am in awe of the fact that kids these days understand the usage of such phrases for being sarcastic and how Anaira used it to her advantage.

Anaira: See Dada, I did this drawing. (they were just a bunch of lines crossing each other)

Me: (being the nice fatherly figure) Oh how beautiful it is, Anaira!

Anaira: Of Course!

Me: Grrrrrrr!

Another instance:

Anaira: Dada, I want to eat.... hmmm.... One teddy bear!

Me: Anaira, are you mad or something!

Anaira: No

Me: How can you eat a teddy bear?

Anaira: Why?

Me: Anaira, get lost! You think I am mad?

Anaira: Of Course!

Me: Grrrrrrr!

Yet another:

Me: Anaira baby, can you please get me my mobile.

Anaira: (searches for it and gets it) Take Dada. I good girl? (Good girl smile)

Me: Yeah right. For such small things, you don't become nice! You should blah blah blah... Do something good... Blah blah..

Anaira (with her head down walks away) I good girl!

Me: Come here baby! You are good girl le my doll!

Anaira: (turns around) Of Course!

Let's wait for TV!

Kids sometimes come up with funny ways of communication. What is even more funnier is how the motherly instinct still understands the meaning of what they are trying to imply. As a father, sometimes, I am clueless and then look at my wife for support to help me understand.

For a change this afternoon, Anaira was feeling hungry and so she asked Soumya if food was ready.

Anaira: Mamma, food is leady?

Mamma: No sweetheart. It will take some more time.

Anaira: Ok Mamma. Let's wait for TV.

At this time, I looked up from the interesting book in my hand, 'Great by Choice'.

Soumya: (looking at my puzzled face) She meant to say that while we are waiting for the food to be cooked, we'll watch TV.

It took 0.5378 seconds for my palm to reach my forehead.

Belt him!

For some reason, Rishaan and Anaira think that I go to office to beat Spiderman and the office pays me for doing this job. Imagine they think that is how I bring the moolah home! (Like I am some Hitman or something)

So this morning, because Anaira's mood was bad while going to school, I reminded her that when she was in school, Dada would beat Spiderman up. Her pretty face brightened up. To add to it, her over enthusiastic brother spoke up.

Rishaan: Dada, you belt him off properly. You catch him and belt him. Then you again belt him.

As he was speaking, his eyes fell on my belt.

Rishaan: You take this belt also and belt him!

Sleeping time!

Kids learn by copying from their surroundings, from what they witness. Again, they speak from their little experiences and exposures that they have had in life.

So after breakfast this morning, Anaira decided that she needed to put me to sleep like the way we used to put her to sleep when she was a baby. So she took me to the room and made me sleep on whatever little of her lap as was available.

As she was patting my head, I suggested that she should sing a song for me to sleep faster.

Anaira: Aisa ludla sa.... (Jiyo Re Bahubali song)

Me: Anaira, are you putting me to sleep or you want me to get up?

Anaira: sorry Dada. (Thinks for two seconds) Dish kamaliya (This was the Twist Kamariya song!)

Me: I am feeling like getting up and dancing

Anaira: (Hushed tone) Dish kamaliya, dish kamaliya....

Poor girl, the recency effect was playing on her! She was singing from what she was exposed to lately.

Susceptible!

Its funny when kids listen to words for the first time. The way they interpret the word in their own way and how they pronounce the word even if it is being repeated; Gosh, kids are cute!

So this one day, Rishaan had got ready for his bath and entered the bathroom. Just to tease me, he behaved as if he was going to slip over a patch of water! I swooshed and reached out to him in 0.736 seconds!

Me: Rishaan, don't do that! You know you are susceptible to falling. Why would you do this?

Rishaan: (ignoring me) I want to go for Potty!

In turn, I ignored him and continued. I had an amusing idea.

Me: Say 'susceptible'!

Rishaan: (mumbled something beyond recognition)

Me: Do you know what is the meaning of susceptible?

Rishaan: No

Me: It means you are prone to. Come let's take bath! Illiterate fellow!

Rishaan: POTTYYY!

Me: Oh sorry!

Rishaan: (losing temper) From that time I am telling potty, potty and you are telling 'susepitle', 'suscepitle'!

Life Lessons

*"Kids don't remember what you try to teach them,
they remember what you are."*

—Jim Henson

Retaliation!

Yesterday, Rishaan got pushed to the ground by one of the small boys in the apartment while playing. As expected of Rishaan's character, he did not retaliate at that moment and let it go.

However the next morning, when he narrated out the incident to me over a conversation, I decided to give him some 'Les Brown' motivation for life. While he was having his breakfast, I saw an opportunity and I told him that if he finished his meal in five minutes, I would accompany him in the evening and we will beat up the guy.

Me: I will catch him by the collar and lift him. Then I will.....

Rishaan: Dada, you catch him. I will kick him from behind.

Me: Wow. I like that. What else will you do?

Rishaan: (aggression increasing) I will make him run and then I will take the cycle and dash him.

Me: Very nice. What else will you do?

Rishaan: (highest form of aggression) I will throw him to the ground and I will sit on him.

Me: Great so can you go to his house and order him to come down?

Rishaan: (after thinking for a while) Errrrr... You come! (with a pleading puppy face)

Ticking Dada!

After the one and a half months of holidays, life has again got back to being super busy. The early morning routines for the kids have returned back to torment them in the form of a father, who is badly wanting to catch up with time.

Sometimes I feel like holding the hands of the clock and yelling out 'STOOOOPPPP!' But then reality bites. We are all meant to be little imperfect people in this maddening world and so it must be!

Enough of philosophy and let's dive into the joke!

Rishaan and Anaira were eating their breakfast as usual. Usual means slooowly! In the meanwhile, with lightning speed, I was running from room to room trying to get their bags and water bottles in place when I stopped and looked at them. Then I looked at the clock.

Me: (raising my voice) Look at the ticking clock! My head is also ticking!

Anaira: What means 'ticking'?

Me: (smoke out of my ears) That tick tick tick sound of the clock is the 'ticking' I am talking about.

Anaira: Oh I see!

Rishaan: Then we will make your face also round and we will put numbers on it. Hands also we will put!

At any other given time, any common man would have laughed at the joke; I buried my head in my palms and screamed as loud as I could! What could I do; I am but a helpless father of two angels who could be childishly mischievous at times.

Fashion Diva

"I don't do fashion. I am fashion."

—Unknown

Put lipstick!

We were getting ready to go out for a ride to our all-time favourite 'Corner House', an ice cream parlour for an evening dessert craving time. We were all set to go when Anaira noticed Soumya at the dressing table.

Anaira: I also want lipstick!

Soumya: Anaira, what did Sonia ma'am say with regards to lipstick? (Anaira's class teacher had actually told her not to wear the lipstick in an attempt to take her mind off the cosmetic)

Anaira: (little liar) Sonia Ma'am said to put!

Soumya: Can I call her and check?

Anaira: (turning away, pissed) It's ok. I don't want lipstick!

Little that she was, Anaira was actually trying her luck to see if there was anything possible and that we might actually fall for her trap through her confident lie. Kids, I tell you!

Dentist – Part 2

As we were seated at the waiting room of the clinic, we were joined by an old couple. This old man was the principal of a school in the vicinity and soon found himself fatally attracted to the brother sister duo.

The old man got particularly interested in Anaira who was busy talking to Rishaan about the colour pencils that the receptionist had given them. He gestured out to her to come close to him and when she was close enough, he asked her for her name. As she was calling out her name, he pulled her off shoulder sleeves to cover the top of her shoulders. I think he thought that the shoulder sleeves had slid off.

Anaira held a hand out asking him to stop. Pulling the sleeves down as they originally were, she told him.

Anaira: (authoritatively) This is like this only!

The dentist, Soumya and I were in a corner covering our mouth with our palms, controlling our laughter.

She removed my lipstick!

On her second day at school, Anaira was still coming to terms with what was happening in her life. One of her all time motivation to do anything at all was lipstick. So when she asked for it in the morning, her ask was granted. (For those of you who must be like, OMG! What are they doing to the little girl, it's lip balm that Soumya applies; something that Anaira does not know. Got an intelligent wife!)

So when Soumya went to pick Anaira off school, Anaira spoke in an irate manner in front of her class teacher.

Anaira: Mamma, this ma'am rubbed off my lipstick.

Ma'am: No darling! You were crying and so I wiped your tears! I didn't touch your lipstick!

Anaira: No Mamma. She rubbed off the lipstick!

Only kids can speak in front of authority with absolutely no fear of the consequences.

Don't want kiss!

I had to take Anaira to the photo studio for her first passport size photo. I had instructed Soumya to get the little lady ready before I reached home.

And sure enough, there she was in her red jacket. Additionally, because she was taking a picture, she had asked Soumya to also put 'Kajal' and lipstick as well.

She was looking so pretty that I couldn't stop myself from carrying her and planting a kiss on her soft cheek. Then I looked at her and requested for a kiss.

Me: Can I get a kiss from the lovely lady?

She kissed me in a way that I didn't feel her lips. So I asked for another one.

Me: I want one kiss.

Anaira: (with twisted lips) I can't give. Lipistick is there!

My eyes popped out; I wasn't getting a kiss because my daughter had applied lipstick. Imagine!

Online shopping!

There's something about the girl child and fashion sense. Maybe sometimes it depends on how much the girl child looks up at her role model; in most cases, her mother and in other cases, a close family friend or relative. Soumya is a very stylish person and always stays abreast with the latest in fashion by ensuring that she allocates enough time in a week to browsing on the fashion sites.

This one night whilst we were preparing to go to sleep, both mother and daughter were busy doing some online shopping on Hopscotch.

Soumya was showing her the dresses and asking her opinion and genuine opinions were being given by the fashion frenzy Anaira. Needless to say, her taste was pretty good. Anaira was actually not liking any of the bad designs and was liking all the good designs.

Anaira stated that one particular dress was very nice. So Soumya turned the mobile screen to show it to me. It was indeed a very pretty polka dot dress. I made an expression that matched the thought that I was indeed impressed. Looking at my expression, Anaira immediately spoke to clarify

Anaira: This is not your dress. This is for me - Anaira dress it is.

I bowed my head and joined my hands in reverence of the holy mother of fashion.

Rishaan from Mars and Anaira from Venus!

Scene 1:

Me: Rishaan, will you be able to guide me in this heavy traffic whilst you are sitting in the front.

Both of us were riding through the Bangalore traffic.

Rishaan: Ok Dada. I will help.

Me: Tell me when to stop and I will stop.

A vehicle comes in the front. Immediately Rishaan reacts.

Rishaan: Dada, STOP!

Scene 2:

Me: Anaira, will you guide Dada through this traffic?

Anaira: Yes Dada. Don't wolly.

A vehicle comes right in front of us. No reaction from Anaira. I hit the brakes.

Me: Anaira, why you didn't tell Dada to stop?

Anaira: What happened, Dada?

Me: We would have dashed that vehicle.

Anaira: I was seeing my nail polish no?

When John Gray (author, Men Are from Mars, Women Are from Venus) would have had the initial idea to write the book which got him on top of the charts across continents, something tells me he was also driving through traffic.

Lipstick Again!

Anaira was eating her meal when Soumya walked out looking all pretty, all decked up to go out for her freelance classes. I complimented her for looking so gorgeous; Anaira however seemed to have her eyes glued on to Soumya's lips for the Maybelline.

Needless to say, the next moment witnessed Soumya handing out a sleek lip gloss to the fashion frenzy Anaira.

The diva got to work with the lip gloss and her lips and with the precision of an artist, she started painting her lips. She was looking so cute as she stood in front of the dressing table that I pinched her cheeks and kissed her. To my surprise, she lost her cool.

Anaira: You mad or what, Dada? Lipstick is in my hand no?

I considered it wise to walk out of the scene. No one messes with the 'Anaira'.

I was not dressed up!

Soumya and I were clearing up the cupboard when we stumbled upon our wedding album. And as any romantic couple, who have made promises of growing old together and the like, we immersed ourselves into the memories of the day that brought us legally together.

In a matter of minutes, we were joined by our offsprings who broke into our little reverie and brought us to our present day. I looked at Anaira and decided to have a conversation.

Me: Anaira, do you know what this is? (Pointing to the album)

Anaira: (very confidently) Yeah!

Me: What is it?

Anaira: This is Mamma Dada marriage.

Me: Anaira, why did you not come for the marriage?

The style conscious diva thought for a while and then spoke.

Anaira: Because I was not dressed up!

Guess, this is a valid enough answer for most of our kids who couldn't make it for our respective marriages.

I'll call Santa?

One of the universal things that most of the parents can instantly connect on is the food habits of their children. Im sure if someone can come up with a solution to that challenge, they'd turn millionaires overnight.

The other day, I was feeding Anaira milk from the glass and after a certain quantity, she started running around the house with me and the glass of milk close to her heels. So I threatened her.

Me: Anaira, I'll call Santa?

Anaira: Ha yes, call and tell, 'Anaira wants one lipistick, one kazal.....

Sometimes, you are pissed off and laughing at the same time. This situation called for me to display that type of an emotion.

Curious Kids

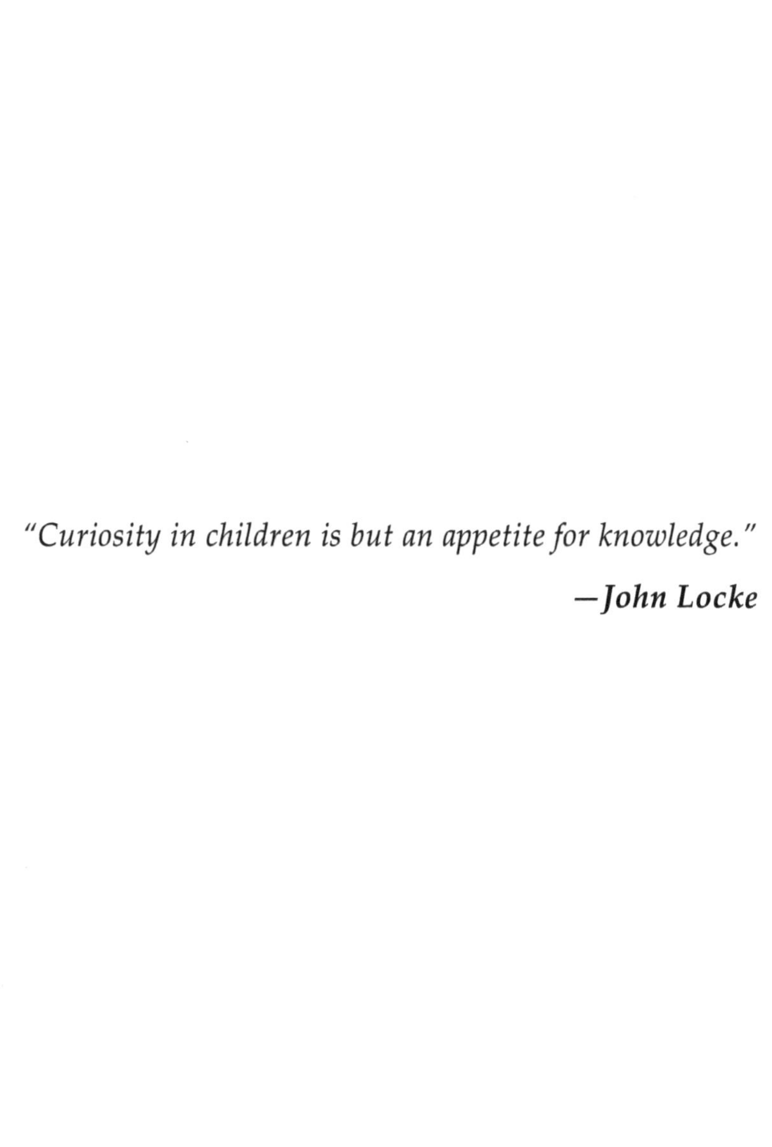

"Curiosity in children is but an appetite for knowledge."

—John Locke

Curiosity killed the cat – Part 1

I know kids are curious, but Rishaan is a league ahead of the rest. For example, we were in the Pilikulu zoo in Mangalore around Christmas and we were getting late to finish the zoo and retire back to our hotel; we still had a long way to go.

Rishaan, on the other hand, wanted to have a glimpse of every single animal, just a glimpse was enough. It started getting on my nerves after a point. So, on a certain occasion, I decided to speak to him.

Me: Rishaan, it is not nice to be so curious in life. Remember that curiosity killed the cat.

Rishaan: Why they killed?

Me: (not expecting that) Errr.. they killed! That's all. So don't be so curious.

Rishaan: Then what should we be?

Aarrrrghhh! Listening to my frustrated roar, I'm sure all the animals in the zoo would have concluded that there was a new animal transported to the zoo that day.

Curiosity killed the cat – Part 2

So now that we know that Rishaan is a very curious child, 'curiouser' than the rest of his friends and their friends, this happened today. But before that you should know something.

A few days back, a cat had killed a big lizard on the steps of our apartment. This was big news in my house as Rishaan and Anaira had to pass the dead lizard whilst on the way to school. I can only imagine what would have been the topic of discussion at their school; being the story tellers that they are.

Anyways, today after Rishaan displayed an eccentric level of curiosity, I reiterated a gem of wisdom.

Me: Rishaan, remember that curiosity killed the cat.

Rishaan: No re. The cat killed the lizard!

I swallowed so hard as I stared at the little boy wonder that for a moment, I felt that I had swallowed the very same gem of wisdom.

Dada's Little Girl

*"A father holds his daughter's hand for a short while,
but he holds her heart forever."*

—Unknown

I don't have anything

Dada and Anaira were on their way back after dropping li'l Rishaan to school whilst listening to the essential collection of John Denver on the car's stereo system. She started an interesting conversation with me.

Background to the conversation: A Spiderman mascot had scared Anaira crazy during the family day gathering organized for all the employees at KPMG Global Services, one of the organisations that I had worked with. Even though I had moved organisations post that, Anaira still believes I am at KPMG and so is Spiderman.

Anaira: When you go to office no Dada, you do dishoom to that Spiderman.

Me: Ok Anaira. But if I do dishoom what will you give me?

Anaira: (putting her head down as if depressed) No nothing Dada.

Me: But I want something, Anaira.

Anaira: (filled with remorse) I don't have anything Dada.

Saying this, she took a step closer and hugged me.

Me: (whilst keeping my eyes on the road) This hug is a lot Anaira, it is a lot.

Anaira: (her lil face brightened) Leally Dada?

Me: Really!

And as if John Denver got a clue out of this little private moment, the famous father daughter song, 'For Baby' began to play its charm out of the speakers adding to the beauty of that moment.

Police!

I had just arrived home and both Rishaan and Anaira were in an ecstatic state to see me home so early. So we all started jumping around like monkeys and celebrating the present moment. As parents, the faster we learn that it is the little things that matter the most, the sooner we learn to enjoy parenthood!

Anyways, as Anaira and I continued doing a tribal dance, Rishaan and Soumya walked inside the room. After a while, I could hear Rishaan laughing out uncontrollably. The reason - Soumya was tickling his smooth little stomach.

This looked like a nice plan to me and I carried Anaira without a warning and I put the sister next to her brother. I was about to start tickling her as well but then I could see that she was already influenced by the contagious laughter from Rishaan. She was already in peels of laughter and this was going to be too much for her to take.

As soon as I brought my fingers closer, without hesitation, she started screaming out:

'POLICE! POLICE!'

I stopped short of tickling her and fell to the floor laughing myself!

Water

One of the biggest trials after a baby enters our life is when the baby cries at night. As a parent, this was one of the greatest challenges for me, someone who loves sleep like nothing else.

It was 3 AM in the night; the Paes' were in the deepest hour of sleep when suddenly Anaira started crying loudly. Whilst Rishaan slumbered on unaffected by the whole occurrence, Soumya and I woke up to action.

Soumya: What happened, baby? You want dudu?

Anaira: Nooooo.. (continues crying louder)

Soumya: You want water?

Anaira: Noooooo (cries even louder making us feel that as parents we do not know her wants well enough)

Soumya: Ok. What do you want?

Anaira: Plain water!

Aargghhhh! As I walked out irritated and sleep deprived to get her the 'plain' water and God knows what she meant by the phrase, one more instruction followed, all of this with eyes closed.

Anaira: Normal water!

Ploblem

I had irritated Anaira enough by pinching her and pulling her little shirt. After a while, she started getting pissed off with me and displayed behaviour that reflected this, making facial expressions that showed disapproval of what I was doing, ignoring me altogether, hitting me back on my leg, etc.

So when I went close to her to ask her if she wanted to eat something after a while, she ignored me. I pushed her gently and asked her, 'What's your problem?'

Without hesitation, she sharply retorted, 'You ploblem!'

Movie Buffs

*"Kids are great actors and pretty natural as well.
Ask me – I have got two of the world's
best in my house."*

—Loyson Paes

Thud!

Anaira was in an extraordinarily energetic mood this one morning. As she unbuttoned her jumpsuit and more and more skin began to show up, she sang the Bahubali theme song with a never seen before aggression.

Anaira: Aisa, ludla sa, hai salvatla samudla sa!

I responded by matching her aggressive expression. She repeated the lyrics till the jumpsuit was off and then dragging the suit, she walked toward the bedroom.

Unfortunately the aggression did not last long. As she walked, her tiny feet got entangled in the jumpsuit. The rest of the task was done by gravity. Thud!

Bahubali's bath

As I poured the first tumbler of water on Rishaan, he screamed aloud that it was hot. Lazy to add cold water to the bucket, I started explaining to Rishaan as I poured out the next tumbler of water.

Me: Rishaan do you know that Bahubali takes bath with water that is 100 degrees centigrade.

Rishaan: Really? Where is his bathroom?

Me: That is not the point. This water is only 50 degrees centigrade.

Rishaan: Oh my God!

Me: Do you understand what that means?

Rishaan: Yes

Me: What do you understand?

Rishaan: (in the same tone) I don't know!

Is it tomorrow today?

On a cozy Sunday morning, as we were watching some TV as a family, Rishaan suddenly sat up.

Rishaan: Is it tomorrow today?

Soumya and I started laughing thinking that this only was the joke. But then he continued.

Rishaan: Yesterday you had said no that Bahubali movie is tomorrow. Tell no, is it tomorrow?

Et Al

"There are no seven wonders of the world in the eyes of a child. There are seven million."

—**Walt Streightiff**

Reached home!

Generally when I reach home, I am greeted by screams and yells from Rishaan and Anaira. This is followed by complaints about each other and self-appreciations.

Yesterday was different.

As I opened the main door, no scream. Anaira was sitting on the floor engrossed in her Lego. She turned to look at me but did not smile. For a second, I felt she was going to cry. I non-verbaled out to her asking what happened. No response. Suddenly she turned back and yelled out to Soumya in the kitchen.

Anaira: Mamma, Dada came.... He reached our home only!

Soumya and I burst out laughing at the choice of words. Rishaan, who was in the other bedroom till then, ran out and the situation was back to screams and yells.

That is other people's concern!

Anaira was punished with her little hands up! I cannot disclose the reason for the punishment as I promised her that stays a secret whilst I took her permission to put this up as a joke! So when her hands started paining, she looked at me with tears rolling down her cheeks.

Anaira: Dada, where is mamma?

Me: (trying hard to be stern inspite of the heavenly cute looks) THAT is not your concern!

Rishaan was somewhere in the bedroom playing and suddenly yelled back.

Rishaan: That is other people's concern!

The next minute saw him standing right next to the punished Anaira with his little hands up as well for speaking out of turn. Unlike Anaira however, he laughed his way through the punishment!

I will give money!

Anaira was creating ruckus making me run behind her to eat. So Soumya made a 'call' to Santa.

Soumya: Hello Santa.

Anaira immediately opened her mouth to gulp in a gallon of milk.

Soumya: Santa, for Anaira we would like her to have one Maybelline lipstick....

Another gallon of milk was consumed.

Soumya: ..... One Colossal Kajal... Bangles.... One thees thees (perfume spray)....

Three gallons down.

Me: Aey stop. Enough with that list!

Anaira: Why?

Me: Because then Santa will send me a bill after delivery. Dada will have to pay money.

Anaira: Dont wolly Dada. I will give money from my piggy bank.

Let me introduce myself to all of you once again. I am the poor dad of a rich daughter.

Snakes and Laddoo

Anaira was with the snakes and ladder board game playing a nonsensical, never-played-before session.

She was climbing up on the snakes tails and climbing down on the ladders and was making noises as she was going up and down the imaginary roads.

Me: What are you playing, Anaira?

Anaira: Snakes and Laddoo!

Had to be Snakes and Laddoo because the Snakes and Ladders that I am aware of is a gentleman's game compared to what I was witnessing.

Thermometer!

4 AM. Soumya woke me up and asked me to check Anaira's temperature manually to see if she had fever. Through my sleepy eyes, I reached out to feel Anaira's forehead and neck and then agreed that she indeed was hot!

Suddenly a tiny angelic voice in the dark was heard, surprisingly loud and clear with no grammatical mistakes whatsoever.

Anaira: Dada, please bring the thermometer and then check.

My sleepy eyes opened big and wide only to see a beautiful pair of eyes on an expressionless face staring back, patiently waiting for me to act on the instruction just delivered.

Discussion on the bike!

Anaira, Rishaan, Niranjan (Soumya's brother) and I were headed out to a little kiddy place so that the kids could have a good time and the adults could get sometime to catch up on topics that needed attention.

Rishaan outran us all and got onto the front part of the Avenger 220 which is generally Anaira's place. Obviously, when Anaira reached the scene, all hell broke loose.

Fortunately or unfortunately, in this situation, I was supposed to be the negotiator. So I began.

Me: Rishaan, wouldn't you like to sit behind Dada with Niranjan and discuss about his college?

Rishaan: No Dada. I want to sit in the front and discuss about KPMG with you.

I turned to look at Anaira, who stared back up at me with folded hands with a ray of hope that this authority called Dada would provide an absolutely unbiased verdict. I felt the same pressure that the Chief Justice of India experienced when about to deliver the verdict on the Ayodhya issue.

Not Anaila, Anaila!

For a very long time, when I was small I remember having difficulty with pronouncing the words that had an 'R' sound in them. Somehow, that 'inability' led to a lot of fine moments that my family fondly remembers even today. Not so much with Rishaan but Anaira has inherited this trait from me.

Soumya was lazing around on the sofa when she noticed Anaira trotting along with her dolls from one bedroom to another.

Soumya: (loving imitation) Anaila baby, come here!

Anaira: (with an intent to correct her) Mamma, not Anaila! (pause) It is Anaila!

Soumya: (smiling) Same thing no baby! Anaila!

Anaira shook her head in disgust and shrugged her shoulders with a look that showed that she did not have too many hopes on Mamma!

Run for my life also!

It is beyond imagination sometimes to think of how a child can think. I mean as adults we have learning sessions on how to think outside the box, but for a child, the box by itself is non-existent. The box grows as we grow up.

Rishaan and I were playing a game involving an imaginary monster. It was like a little skit and we had to make a run as soon as the breeze moves the curtain assuming that the monster had entered. It was fun. Sometimes the most nonsensical games seem fun when kids are involved.

At this one point, the curtain moved and I screamed out the first:

Me: Oh My Gosh! Run for your life!

Rishaan: (running) Run for my life also!

Like only a child can think like this. I fell on the ground hard as I burst out laughing at the thought process.

Don't tell all that!

Kids can have an ego that is much bigger than the very bodies that they possess. This is clearly seen from the likes and dislikes, the way they behave in front of other people and the like.

On our way out from the house to have a private little celebration for Soumya's birthday, we bumped into our immediate neighbours who love talking to Rishaan. So once Rishaan had revealed the whole fuss about the secret dinner, all thanks to his loud mouth, the neighbours decided to interrogate him a little more on this topic.

They: What did you give for mamma on her birthday?

Soumya: Troubles! He troubled me the entire day.

Rishaan: (very slowly so only Soumya could hear) Don't tell all that, mamma! It is our inside house matter.

I like your wife too!

On a lazy morning, Soumya, Rishaan and I were sitting down and having a chat when Rishaan suddenly raised his voice with Soumya over an argument. I immediately interrupted and spoke firmly. Its always better to draw and show the line to the kids when they cross it.

Me: Rishaan, you dont speak to my wife like that. I love my wife! And I will not tolerate anyone speaking to her like that.

Seeing the situation rolling out of control, Rishaan confidently smiled and responded as he playfully jumped over Soumya.

Rishaan: Even I love your wife!

Its amazing how kids can even win lost battles.

So are you mad?

Weekends are complete family time. As you can imagine Soumya and I are super busy over the weekdays and operate very mechanically as we get the kids ready to get to school and closing in on the daily chores and the office work. Hence weekends get to be life savers as they let us be our human selves once again.

Rishaan and Anaira love going over to meet their cousins so we make sure there is a reunion periodically and whenever feasible. As I was driving to my sister's place with the family this one weekend, Rishaan complained to me about Anaira.

Rishaan: See Dada, Anaira is calling me mad fellow.

Me: (philosophical mode) Hmmmm! Rishaan, it is ok when some one calls you mad because remember we all need a little bit of madness to get what we want in life. So by those standards, you should say 'thank you' to Anaira when she calls you mad.

I paused for the little brains to absorb the deep thought. Then continued.

Me: So, are you mad?

Rishaan: (Loud and clear) Yes Dada.

Soumya: (bursting the bubble tone) Chheee Rishaan, you are mad?

Rishaan: (as if out of a hypnotherapy) Aey, no mama!

Soumya was able to snap Rishaan out of a trance that I had motivationally created for him. I guess that's the power of a mother's love.

Choco Pie baby

Kids can be really creative and if they are let to be themselves without any boundaries, forget the box; they would have no box at all.

For quite a while, Anaira was very fond of the new song, 'Rock-a-bye baby' by Clean Bandit. The other day, whilst she was eating a Choco Pie, we heard her quietly singing to herself, 'Choco-pie baby Choco-pie, I'm gonna rock you....'

Guessing she got confused between the song and the delicacy or was it her simple creativity? Ahem!

I good girl!

A lovely Sunday morning called for a little bike ride to the nearby market and thus the Paes clan set out! After buying all the items needed for the Paes' residence, we came back to the bike but Anaira created a ruckus as she didn't want Rishaan to come back on the bike. So Soumya and Rishaan decided to walk back after making faces at Anaira for the pain she was.

I rode back with Anaira setting out a little lecture on the way in which she was obviously not interested. As soon as we reached home, we caught up with the rest of the family on the steps.

Soumya: Dada, Rishaan and I not talking to you

Me: Mamma, I am sorry. I good boy?

Soumya: Yes Dada. You good boy. I talk to you.

Three feet below us, we heard a little fighter pacify herself.

Anaira: I good girl!

Anaira in this case was absolutely certain of her 'good' self. Oh, how I wish the belief that a child has in herself stays forever.

Planets of the Solar System!

The conversations at the Paes residence these days have been circulating around Science, Animals and the Solar system. And boy, am I enjoying it! I am learning so much more than the kids.

There are such lovely videos for kids on YouTube that I am getting to know them only now. An animated line of planets introduce themselves in a song, an animated uncle talking about how volcanoes erupt and what not!

Anyways, so I have been getting the kids to memorise the names of the 8 planets these days and we generally do this on the way to school.

Me: So let's take the names of the planets? Mercury (both repeat), Venus (both repeat), Earth (both repeat), blah blah, Neptune (both repeat). Good boys and girls! Now you say?
Rishaan: Mercury, Errr, ... January, February, ...

A nearby street dog jumped out of its skin as Dada roared with laughter with a two second delay and subsequent laughter from the kids!

Go to sleep!

Through a very usual tiresome day at the Paes' residence, on the bed, there lay two 'tired beyond their senses' adults and two 'raving to go for another shift energy packed' toddlers who were forced against their will to sleep.

So Soumya started telling them a story in the hope that they would go to sleep. High hopes, I agree but always worth a try in parenthood!

After struggling to stay awake through the story herself, Soumya also explained the moral of the story. Then Anaira pats my pretty wife's forehead.

Anaira: Now go to sleep. It is late!

Sometimes frustration beyond a limit lets you let out a giggle; a giggle of absolute helplessness.

Don't talk to her!

Rishaan was playing in the Children's Play area in the apartment. One of his friends was on the swing with her dad standing behind pushing her along. Rishaan walks up to her.

Rishaan: Come let's play on the see saw.

Girl: No. I want to play on swing.

Rishaan: Come leave the swing. Let's play on the see saw.

Girl: No. I want to swing.

Rishaan (irate; looks at her dad and says): Don't talk to her. Bad girl she is.

Girl's dad: Arey, she is my daughter. Why should I stop talking to her?

Rishaan (closing statement tone): Because she is a bad girl!

All the parents in the park were in peals of laughter as the dumbstruck father looked on.

Jackets

Last night, whilst on the way to relish an ice cream at Corner House, a conversation between my pretty wife and the legend

Soumya: What do cows give us?

Rishaan: Cows give us dudu!

Soumya: Very good. What do dogs give us?

Rishaan: Security and protect our houses

Soumya: Very good. You deserve a jelly. Ok, what do sheep give us

Rishaan: Jackets!

And we laughed and ROFLed all the way to the Corner House and beyond!

Train track

Rishaan brought this drawing of a train track to Soumya and me.

Rishaan: See Mamma, train!

Soumya: But where is the train, Rishaan?

Rishaan: (Spontaneously) See on the track. Now it's gone. You should see fast no.

This is the first time in Soumya's lifetime that someone had asked her to be fast.

I firmly believe that every house has a similar story, that we have humour, laughter and wit in every child. I would love to listen to the 'parental bloopers' taking place within the four walls of your house and beyond.

Whilst I have started work on the second book, I would love for the subsequent books of *Parental Bloopers* to have stories from your home. Do feel free to write to me directly at loysonwrites@gmail.com and I'd love to compile the best into a manuscript someday.

Your Child. Your Story. Parental Bloopers – Vol x.

Loy ☺